YOU ARE MORE THAN A CONQUEROR

ROMANS 8:37

Prophetic Evangelist
CARLENE KERR MATHEWS
Foreword by Dr. Bob Rodgers

First Paperback edition, March, 2025

Manufactured in the United States of America
ISBN: 979-8-9917464-0-3 (Paperback)
ISBN: 979-8-9917464-1-0 (eBook)

Contents

Acknowledgments. v

Foreword. vii

Chapter 1: A Heritage of Faith 1

Chapter 2: Prayer and Revelation. 11

Chapter 3: Wisdom 25

Chapter 4: Angels on Assignment. 31

Chapter 5: Perfect Timing. 37

Chapter 6: Will You Obey Him?. 45

Chapter 7: Our Daily Bread 53

Chapter 8: Set Your Minds 59

Chapter 9: Bearing Fruit and Having Abundant Life 75

Chapter 10: Fast, Fasted, Fasting 79

Chapter 11: Heal, Healed, Healing: The Healer in You . . 87

Chapter 12: Make the Choice to Rejoice 93

Chapter 13: Our Hearts. 101

Chapter 14: Seek His Kingdom 111

Chapter 15: Humility 117

Chapter 16: Our Words 125

Chapter 17: Women in the Bible................... 131

Chapter 18: Use Your Authority 137

Chapter 19: More Than a Conqueror 143

About the Author............................... 153

Acknowledgments

The beloved husband of my youth, Thomas N. Mathews, who is truly my greatest supporter and is now cheering me on from the heavens.

My Godly Parents, Pastor Willliam Carlos Kerr & Mrs. Fonta Bel Kerr

The late Pastor W. L. Rodgers

Brother, Pastor Rudd Alen Kerr

Production and Publishing Supervisor, April Driskell

Typist and Preliminary Editor, Jana Morgan

Aunt, Mildred L Kerr

Cousin, Patricia Gannon

Daisy Stevenson

Iva Coffee

Foreword

"You are More than a Conqueror" is the story of the legacy of Carlene Mathews. Carlene was the daughter of a Baptist preacher that instilled in her the Word of God, integrity, hard work and the understanding of the power of prayer.

These attributes enabled Carlene to become one of the most powerful intercessors and soul winners I have ever met in over forty years of ministry. Of the hundreds that she has led to the Lord, she also mentored them where they became leaders and led hundreds of others to Christ as well.

"You are More than a Conqueror" is the story of how God can use you to bring a supernatural favor and increase on not only you and your family, but upon numerous others you come in contact with.

Dr. Bob Rodgers
Evangel World Prayer Center
ewpc.com

CHAPTER 1

A Heritage of Faith

I am Audrey Carlene Kerr Mathews, born in Grayson County, Leitchfield, Kentucky. I was the fourth child and youngest of three daughters born to William Carlos Kerr and Fonta Bel Hartley Kerr. My daddy did some cattle trading with my papa, Lawrence Hartley, who came from Tipera, Ireland. That's when Daddy spotted my mother, who was only sixteen and a sophomore attending Clarkson High School. She was kind of tall, long-legged, with dark hair and beautiful blue eyes. My daddy decided that she was the pretty gal with whom he wanted to spend the rest of his life. He was nine-and-a-half years older than mother; she was only sixteen while he was twenty-five. Some folks would say that he "robbed the cradle."

After two years of marriage, my oldest brother was born. My mother had a great-uncle whom she was fond of named Rudd, so they decided their first-born baby boy would be named Rudd Allen. My parents were in their small apartment in Highland Park, Louisville, Kentucky when mother went into labor. They called a taxi cab and off they went to the old Baptist hospital where Rudd was born, with the well-known 1937 flood in full force on their way.

Two years later, Mother gave birth to a beautiful, red-headed baby girl. My grandmother was a redhead, although Mother and her siblings, Ola and Herman, didn't have red hair. Many times it skips a generation. My parents decided to name their second child Peggy Louise. The "Louise" came from my dad's sister, Aunt Mildred Louise. Two years later my sister Temple was born. She had very dark black hair and beautiful blue eyes. Then when Temple was a few months shy of her second birthday, I was born. Travis Clinton followed when I was two years old, and when he was about two, the youngest of my parents' six children, Carlos Daniel, was born. Mother certainly had her hands full with all six of us so close in age.

After Rudd and Peggy were born, Mom and Dad decided they needed to leave the city of Louisville for Grayson County, Kentucky. The last four of their children were born there on a farm that Dad purchased just two miles outside the city limits of a town called

Leitchfield. It was great fun roaming the hills and fields of the farm with my siblings and cousins. We helped milk the cows and fed our beautiful gray mares Bess and Bert, who were oh so gentle. We would ride them to the water branch nearby.

This may make me sound ancient, but starting when I was four or five my mother was my kindergarten teacher. She would copy her name and Daddy's, printing them and each of my sibling's names as well. Mother would be ironing one of Daddy's white shirts with the old heavy iron and I would be right there asking her to print these family names.

Neither one of my parents had experienced the gift of salvation at the time of their getting married. My daddy had been somewhat of a rebel, and did a lot of drinking and fighting. Daddy grew up with three brothers, and remembers that from the time he was young, his own father, Samuel Kerr, saw God's call on his life. When my grandfather would introduce his sons, he would say about Daddy, "This one is my preacher." He planted seeds of truth and faith in that small four or five year old heart that Dad's calling in life was to preach the glorious Gospel. Now he did lots of running from God's call upon his life, but he also saw glimpses of it. I remember his sharing about being employed in his younger years as a caretaker for a man named John Samuels.

When John was dying, he screamed very loudly, "Take my feet out of these flames of fire!" That certainly left an impression on my dad. And after he became a father himself, his life made a drastic change.

As a child, I remember hearing the story of my Daddy's spiritual rebirth. He and his cousin were out one day running around as a couple of young men and came upon a revival. They heard the Good News of the gospel, and an altar call was made by a preacher known as "Coot" Meredith. Dad's cousin, Guy Kerr, got up and ran out of the back door of this small General Baptist Church. My father later said, "I reached for my hat to run also and found myself at the altar weeping with tears of heart-wrenching repentance." He was so thrilled with the gift of salvation that the following morning he was giving his testimony to everyone in Leitchfield, Kentucky who would listen. It was Election Day, so the crowds were much larger than usual. In years past, Daddy's lifestyle would have had him spending this day drinking alcohol and telling everyone to vote for his favorite candidate. Now he had tasted the new wine that a born again believer experiences, and he had great excitement about being that new creature in Christ Jesus, and sharing with others about God's mercy and grace.

Oh, how very, very thankful I am that my daddy surrendered his life to the Lord Jesus Christ before my younger brothers and I were born. It was a short time later that my mother was gloriously saved. She was born again by the awesome work of the Holy Spirit in the barn where she and Daddy lived and their six children played.

I've told many people that I grew up on "cornbread and Jesus." I'm so very thankful that my parents received Jesus Christ as their personal Savior and knew the importance of taking us to Sunday School and church. The preparation started on Saturday night. We all got our bath in rain water, which was caught outside our farmhouse in tubs because we had no bathroom at the time. We girls had very shiny clean hair after these baths, and so did our brothers. We did not have electricity when I was young either, so we were still using oil lamps for a while. It was very exciting for all of us to eventually use electric lamps and other small appliances.

Every Sunday we would bring home small cards from church with a colorful picture and a Bible verse, sometimes Old Testament and sometimes New Testament. When our parents would read their Bibles they would stress the importance of daily prayer and putting His Word in our hearts and souls.

I remember like it was yesterday that Daddy would come home from the fields and get his old battery-run radio, turning it on to a preacher. I don't remember his name, but he would come on the air speaking Romans 1:16 (KJV) "For I am not ashamed of the Gospel of Christ: for it is the power of God unto salvation to every one that believeth; to the Jew first, and also to the Greek."

I was four years old, and that anointed man of God quoting that Holy Scripture went right past my young mind into my heart and never left me. I often share that I preached my first sermon as a four-year-old on a stump in my cousin's yard. I called out "Repent or perish!" That message stayed with me even at age four. Little children have a tenderness, purity, and innocence that our Heavenly Father loves. I believe I truly might have experienced being "born again" but I had heard many older folks discussing converts, and whether little children coming forward to receive Jesus really knew what they were doing. I decided that when I answered the call to be born again, they would know that I understood the choice I was making.

Our social life growing up usually involved church activities such as picnics. We also had "Decoration Sundays" throughout the county. That's when we would honor those who had gone on to Heaven by decorating their graves. I would invite my best friend, Hilda Buress, from the very small community called Big Clifty. I had friends from my Sunday school class, but

Hilda was one of my friends from school. She too was a follower of Jesus Christ, and so were my friends Betty Lou Harrison and Brenda Carter as well as others. On picnic days we would always have Sunday School, then hear preaching in the mornings and have a picnic on the church grounds in the afternoon with gospel singing groups performing. The meals that everyone enjoyed were made up of delicious veggies grown out of everyone's gardens. I am very grateful that my Awesome, All-Faithful, Gracious Heavenly Father predestined my life to be born in small town U.S.A. in the little state of Kentucky. Of course it did not seem small to me growing up.

We all learn by example. I remember waking in the early morning and hearing Mother and Daddy speaking of God's faithfulness and His goodness toward them and us children. It was also a highlight when, on a special occasion in the summer, there would be singing from the courthouse. We could hear quartets and families singing beautiful songs such as "How Great Thou Art," "Blessed Assurance," and "Rock of Ages". And of course, there was always the famous "Amazing Grace," still many folks' very favorite hymn.

Even when we were dead because of our sins, he gave us life when he raised   Christ from the dead. (It is only by God's grace that you've been saved!) For he raised us up from the dead along with Christ and seated us with him in heavenly realms because we are united with Christ Jesus. (Ephesians 2:5-6)[1]

Years ago, my husband, Tom, and I went to see the movie *Amazing Grace.* It tells the true story of the man who penned this beloved hymn. He had witnessed parents being pulled away from their crying children during the time of slavery. It makes me think of this passage from Ephesians about God's truly amazing grace. The truth from the Word tells us that you and I are seated with Jesus Christ through His gift of salvation!

I was thirteen years of age when I went to the altar, repented of my sin, and received Jesus Christ as my own personal Savior. I was water baptized in a creek in Grayson County, Kentucky, and soon after began ninth grade at Clarkson High School. I was elected beauty queen in my senior year, with Ronnie Grant elected king. Needless to say, I was thrilled, and my dear mother, so full of the good Holy Spirit, was equally excited for me. She found me a beautiful red formal, since we were known as the Red Hawks, and our school colors were red and white or red and black. It was also a big deal to me to

---

[1] Holy Bible, New Living Translation

be elected cheerleader. Our Bibles tell us that we are to "give honor to whom honor is due"[2], and I am very grateful to Hilda for working with me for my tryout cheer. She was very diligent and continued to train me with patience, even though I had hardly any rhythm. Thank you, Lord Jesus, for Hilda! We remained friends, and she and her husband, J. T. Skaggs, were born again believers as well.

I will always remember the last alumni banquet I attended with my sweet husband of my youth, because J. T. and Hilda hosted a get together at their home afterward. It was great fun for all of us. When J. T. Left for Heaven, Hilda only lived a few more years herself. I know, without any doubt, that when I arrive in that Glorious Heaven, our eternal home, they both will be there.

I write this book and share my story, dear heart reader, that you would know you are truly more than a conqueror, regardless of what you may be experiencing in your circumstances. In every situation, we can and should remind ourselves about our Lord's great faithfulness. He is who He says He is. Our Father is truly a very present help at all times, and He tells us the Greater One lives in us (1 John 4:4).

---

[2] Rom 13:7 (Amplified Bible, Classic Edition)

CHAPTER 2

Prayer and Revelation

After graduating from high school, I packed my suitcase and left small town USA. I moved in with my sister, Peggy Louise, and brother-in-law, Buddy, and entered Town and Country Beauty School on Dixie Highway in Louisville, Kentucky. Almost all of the students were fresh out of high school like me, with maybe half a dozen older gals from smaller towns south of Louisville as well. We elected class officers and I was glad to be chosen as president. Our instructors were not Believers and neither were some of the students. I prayed for them. A highlight from my time in beauty school was that my Aunt Ruby lived just a few miles away, so she became a weekly client for me. I also enjoyed working on the mannequins for practice. At the time, we only had to have 900 hours of experience to receive our license to work for a year as an apprentice.

Then we would receive a license to be a full-fledged beauty operator.

My oldest brother, Rudd, was much more involved in my life even than Daddy, who was busy with farming and working construction and holding revival meetings. Thank you, Lord Jesus, that the call of God was so very real and precious in him and was passed down to Rudd and me to be voices for the Glorious Kingdom of God and to surrender daily to His bidding.

In February of 1965, I was at a ministry event when I first saw a certain young man across the room. He noticed me too, and we caught each other's eye a few times until he finally approached me and asked if I would go downstairs and have a Coke with him. Fresh out of three-and-a half-years in the Marine Corps, he had the most beautiful blue eyes, and I thought to myself that I'd likely go almost anywhere with this man! Tom asked for my number that night, and while I didn't give him my home number, I did give him the one for my sister's salon where I worked. The first time he asked me for a date I already had plans, but then he asked if I would go with him to his sister's house for a hayride and I thought that sounded like fun. Six months later, we were standing at the altar of the Baptist church saying, "I do."

Our wedding day was a beautiful, God-touched event. Daddy walked me down the aisle, but I also wanted to have my mother participate, so she joined us both for the last several steps. My oldest brother, Rudd, performed the ceremony, which was so special to me. My sister, Peggy, was my Maid of Honor. I regret now that I didn't include Temple in the wedding party. I think at the time we didn't get along the best, although we became good friends later in life. Tom's sister, Susan, was our little flower girl, and we had a beautiful archway of fresh pink and white carnations. It was a wonderful day.

Our first son, Thomas Keith, was born on Mother's Day. What a gift! Never will I ever have a better one. He gave his life to the Lord Jesus Christ at a small church in Louisville, Kentucky when he was only about four or five years old. We had gone to see the movie, *The Cross and the Switchblade*, the life story of Niki Cruz. An altar call was made at the close of the movie and Tom Keith went forward. My daddy, William Carlos Kerr, water baptized him in a small pond in Butler County, Kentucky where Daddy was pastoring at that time. Our youngest son, John Carlos, was about four or five in Vacation Bible School when he gave his life to the Lord Jesus Christ and was water baptized.

It is of utmost importance that we as parents set the example of being in love with the Lord Jesus Christ, choosing to be a student of God's Word and taking our children to Sunday School and church. I've heard a few folks say, "Don't do as I do, just do what I say." You have to know that doesn't work!

When Thomas Keith was young, I was working as a hairdresser in the Gardenor Lane Shopping Center about twenty minutes from our home. However, I began to call on the Lord for a beauty shop much closer to where we lived, and closer to the Craig family, whose name the Lord had given me to watch Thomas Keith while I worked. They were excellent caregivers and so loved him. Not long after praying that prayer, our neighbor, Jan Painter, approached me. I had been styling her and her mother's hair pieces, which were very popular at that time. Big hair was very much in style. Jan said, "Would you make a trip with me?" Her plan was for us to fly to South Carolina and purchase all the equipment needed to open up a beauty salon. Jan and her husband had leased a building next door to his establishment, Jim's Tavern, which was only about five minutes from our home. I knew right then that my Father had answered my prayer.

Jan said she didn't want to fly to South Carolina without me. I said, "Jan, if the plane were to crash, the gift of salvation that I have would not help you. You would need to receive Jesus Christ as your very own personal Savior." During this same time she asked me, "Carlene, will you pray that we get our liquor license renewed?" I said "Jan, I will pray," knowing that my prayer would actually be for Jan, Jim, their children, and her parents and siblings to experience being born again.

We made the trip to South Carolina and ordered four shampoo bowls, eight hair dryers, and five or six hair stations. All of this was shipped to 4121 Pinecroft Drive, Louisville, Kentucky. We opened up this new beauty salon with a bang, advertising on the Preston Drive-in Theater near the salon. Jan's mother's name was Ann, so our business name was Jan Ann's Coiffures. We had our uniforms made, and each hairdresser wore the same color each day; red, purple, blue, pale green, or lavender. Most of them were jumpsuits worn with white turtlenecks.

This story is a reminder that prayer has great power. The Lord is saying to you through this book, "I delight in answering your prayers."

Genesis 32:29 tells us, "Jacob asked Him and said, "Tell me, I pray Thee, Thy name, and He said, wherefore is it that thou dost ask after My name?" And He blessed Him there."[3]

---

[3] King James Version

In Psalm 2:8, our Heavenly Father says "Ask of Me, and I shall give thee the heathen for thine inheritance, and the uttermost parts of the earth for thy possession."[4] In Zechariah 10:1, the Word says "Ask ye of the Lord rain in the time of the latter rain; so the Lord shall make bright clouds, and give them showers of rain, to everyone grass in the field."[5]

Looking then at the New Testament, Jesus said to His disciples, "Keep on asking, and you will receive what you ask for. Keep on seeking and you will find. Keep on knocking, and the door will be opened to you."[6] When we pray, we have the ear of our Lord. Our Bibles tell us we also have an ear to hear what the Spirit says.

I remember quite well crying out in prayer for one of my special girlfriends, and the Holy Spirit spoke to my heart very clearly these words, "She's being half-hearted in her relationship with Me. I am going to pull the rug out from under her and you will witness her quick brokenness until her whole heart desires of Me." Of course this happened just as the Holy Spirit described it to me. Your Heavenly Father, in all of His deep devotion and amazing love for you and me, will

---

[4] KJV
[5] KJV
[6] NLT

allow uncomfortable happenings and circumstances to take place in our lives to get our attention.

Our awesome Heavenly Father so desires us to have a revelation from Our King, Our Lord and Savior, the Lord Jesus Christ, that if we have been born again, passed from death unto Life, our hearts of stone are turned into hearts of flesh. We are not our own. We were purchased by His precious blood. God the Father, God the Son, God the Spirit, three in One. They have found their home in our hearts through this new birth. Dr. Billy Graham preached this glorious gospel all over the world teaching that you may be a so-called pastor or evangelist or Sunday School teacher, but if you have not experienced being born again by the Spirit, you will be turned into the everlasting eternal hell fire when you die.

In Old Testament days, only the shedding of blood freed God's people from their sins. Killing animals (often spotless lambs) was symbolic of the precious Lamb of God – Jesus Christ yet to come. His blood frees us. That's why we can all sing out, "Oh, the Blood, what can wash away my sins? Nothing but the blood of Jesus!"[7] And it is why we can freely come before our Heavenly Father in prayer.

---

[7] "History of Hymns: 'Nothing but the Blood.'" Discipleship Ministries. December 16, 2019. https://www.umcdiscipleship.org/resources/history-of-hymns-nothing-but-the-blood.

It's never been about church membership. I believe in church membership but it does not give any of us this glorious gift of salvation. Neither does water baptism. But I do believe the Bible teaches us that after the new birth, the immersion into a watery grave is the supreme example Jesus Christ gave as He was baptized by John the Baptist in the Jordan River.

> And when Jesus was baptized, He went up at once out of the water; and behold, the heavens were opened, and he (John) saw the Spirit of God descending like a dove and alighting on Him.

> And behold, a Voice from heaven said, "This is my Son, My Beloved, in whom I delight!"[8] (The King James Version writes "in whom I am well pleased.")

I love how Mark's Gospel starts this way: "The beginnings [of the facts] of the Good News (the Gospel) of Jesus Christ, the Son of God. Just as it is written in the prophet Isaiah: Behold, I send my messenger before your face, who will make ready Your way."[9] In verse

---

[8] Matt 3:16-17 (AMPC)
[9] Mk 1:1-2 (AMPC)

8 of this same chapter, John the Baptist says, "I have baptized you with water, but He (Jesus) will baptize you with the Holy Spirit."

Do you love that Scripture promise? This promise is for every Believer, not just for a chosen few. Our Savior, Jesus Christ, will baptize us with the Holy Spirit!

When I shared with my precious husband of my youth, Thomas, about being baptized in the Holy Spirit, he was good with that report. He made the remark that if people could believe that God parted the Red Sea and brought the walls of Jericho down, surely He could and would give us the gift of speaking in other tongues, languages that we had not learned out of a book. I have spoken about this in different states and cities where my Awesome Heavenly Father opens doors, whether it be radio or television, very small audiences or rather large ones, sharing this gift that our Father has predestined and preordained. I proclaimed this promise before leaving Kentucky and while being paid as a Zone Pastor for the amazing founders of Evangel World Prayer Center, Pastor W. L. and Fern Rodgers.

The Lord eventually opened a great door of opportunity in Texas, where W. L. and Fern had long ago met at Bible College, for our first-born son, Tom, who is an Environmental Chemist, and the wife of his youth, Tonya Carol Williams. Tom and Tonya attended Southern High

School together, where she invited Tom to be her escort to her Junior Prom, and then again for her Senior Prom. Tonya was a straight A student and cheerleader. Tom was a straight A student and quarterback for the high school football team. How very thankful I am that Tonya's parents were Believers. She too was brought up in the church and, like Tom, was baptized in water and also in the Holy Spirit. When Tom left for the University of Kentucky, he was one year ahead of Tonya. She had her own car and worked part time in the Jefferson Mall in Okolona, where she and her family lived. They became husband and wife, and have given my husband and me two beautiful grand darlings who know Jesus Christ as their very own personal Savior. Shelby Peyton, Tom and Tonya's oldest child, was born in Louisville, Kentucky and graduated from Cy Woods High School with all kinds of honors – top ten in a graduating class of nine hundred. Shelby's younger brother, Pierce Thomas, was born three years after her in Houston, Texas. I am so very thankful to the Lord Jesus Christ for His many answered prayers in our lives.

At the very young age of four, John Carlos was already sharing his faith—witnessing to both adults and children. During that time, I was working as a hairstylist and had Sundays through Wednesdays off. Tom Keith was in kindergarten, so I would take John Carlos to a Christian daycare during the days I worked.

There was one little boy who adored John so much that he would cry on the days John wasn't there. John was always so friendly with the other children—they truly enjoyed his presence. He absolutely loved his Sunday School teachers, and they surely loved him in return. That favor from Heaven remained on his life through all his grade school years.

His classmates consistently elected him as class president, year after year. He made very good grades and genuinely enjoyed being a student. Around the age of four, he also began bouncing a basketball. His older brother, Tom Keith, was seven at the time. Their special daddy, Tom, took a portion of the backyard, poured concrete, and put up a basketball goal so they could play.

Tom Keith and his friends would often play together, and little John would do whatever he could to be part of the game. By middle school, John was one of the five starting players on the basketball team, and he continued as a starter all throughout high school.

His dedication paid off—John was awarded a scholarship to play college basketball at Oral Roberts University. Our beloved Pastor Bob Rodgers, himself an ORU graduate, was someone God used to help make that happen. John enjoyed his time at ORU and made good friends there.

Still, he desired to be closer to home—and his brother, his daddy, and I shared that desire too. So in his sophomore year, he made a change. He even became a cheerleader for the team before transferring to Western Kentucky University, where he became a walk-on player.

There, he met and married a cheerleader, Melissa Graviss, and together they had a beautiful baby boy: Jett Carter Mathews. Although they later divorced, they continue to honor and appreciate one another's love for Jett and remain united in supporting him.

Our Heavenly Father's great love for mankind reminds us, as Romans 8:37 says, that we are called to be more than conquerors. John has experienced much success, and his son Jett has followed in his footsteps—always making very good grades. He is currently a junior in college in Manhattan, Kansas.

Because of distance and John's job with Standard Textile, which required quite a bit of travel, Tom and I have not been part of John and Jett's daily lives in the way we would have loved to be.

Even so, I deeply appreciate our glorious Heavenly Father's way of making each of us wonderfully unique. Though Tom Keith and John Carlos share the same parents, their personalities are quite different. John is outgoing and full of energy—so much like me—while

Tom Keith is more reserved, taking after his daddy, the beloved husband of my youth. I have always been the more expressive one, and it brings me joy to see that part of myself reflected in John. We choose to rejoice in the beautiful way our Father has designed each of us, with our own special gifts and ways of being.

It is the desire and cry of my heart that you, the reader, will walk away with a new confidence—knowing that you have been gifted and uniquely equipped by your loving Heavenly Father.

You are more than a conqueror.

CHAPTER 3

Wisdom

I have thought many times about how much we, as disciples of Christ Jesus, disciple our children. The Three-in-One far supersedes our abilities to be wise, gentle, and firm parents. Our Father's Love for us is so very great that He disciplines us and yes, He will chasten or chastise us for our very own good. Deuteronomy 8:5 says, "Thou shalt also consider in thine heart, that, as a man chasteneth his son, so the Lord thy God chasteneth thee."[10] And we can all learn and receive great teachings from King Solomon's proverbs before his horrible fall. "Chasten thy son while there is hope."[11]

In 2 Corinthians, we find an amazing passage describing us as true Believers, desiring to have it our

---

[10] KJV
[11] Prv 19:18 (KJV)

Heavenly Father's way. We choose to rejoice because we belong to our Lord, Master and Keeper of our souls.

> As unknown, and yet well known; as dying and, behold, we live; as chastened, and not killed. As sorrowful, yet always rejoicing; as poor, yet making many rich; as having nothing, and yet possessing all things.[12]

These passages from Hebrews and Proverbs should thrill our hearts about who our Heavenly Father truly is to us:

> And ye have forgotten the exhortation which speaketh unto you as unto children. My son, despise not thou the chastening of the Lord, nor faint when thou art rebuked of Him: For whom the Lord loveth He chasteneth, and scourgeth every son whom He receiveth.13

> For whom the Lord loveth, He correcteth; even as a father the son in whom he delighteth.[14]

---

[12] 2 Cor 6:9-10 (KJV)
[13] Heb 12:5-6 (KJV)
[14] Prv 3:12 (KJV)

The world calls good "evil" and evil "good." God's wisdom and our surrender will bring us into His purpose and plan for our lives. I am reminded of these beautiful verses in Proverbs 2:1-4:

> My son, if thou wilt receive my words, and hide my commandments with thee; So that thou incline thine ear unto wisdom and apply thine heart to understanding; Yea, if thou criest after knowledge and liftest up thy voice for understanding; If thou seekest her as silver, and searchest for her as hid treasures; Then shalt thou understand the fear of the Lord, and find the knowledge of God.[15]

When Tom and I were still living in Louisville with our sons, I was fasting and took a walk. The voice of the Holy Spirit inside of me spoke "Read Proverbs 8." Please, special child of God, called and anointed chosen to be His mouthpiece, His hands and feet, get your Bible and read Proverbs 8. The Lord will speak to you about true wisdom. We tend to think of wisdom as being "soundness of judgment" or "a right use of knowledge." These are some definitions, but the Hebrew idea of

---

[15] KJV

wisdom covers all of life. Wisdom (hokmah) is derived from the verb "hakam" meaning "to be wise or to act wisely." All of the ancient Near East was interested in being wise, so a large body of what we call "wisdom literature" built up in that part of the world during that time.

> And God gave Solomon wisdom and understanding exceeding much, and largeness of heart, even as the sand that is on the seashore.
>
> And Solomon's wisdom excelled all the children of the east country, and all the wisdom of Egypt.[16]

Solomon won the hearts of the people through the situation of two women, one whose baby had died, and both of whom were claiming a live baby was their own. Solomon said, "Let's just cut this live baby in two parts." The true mother was revealed as she screamed out, "Oh, no!" Solomon's wisdom saved a life and uncovered the truth.[17]

This world puts much emphasis on education and that can be a good thing. But true wisdom doesn't come

---

[16] 1 Kgs 4:29-30 (KJV)
[17] 1 Kgs 3:16-28

from a degree. And it brings a deep understanding that goes far beyond books. Proverbs 23:23 tells us to "Buy the truth, and sell it not; also wisdom, and instruction, and understanding."[18]

Charles Dickens said, "A loving heart is the truest wisdom." And Proverbs 11:12 teaches that "He that is void of wisdom despiseth his neighbor, but a man of understanding holdeth his peace."[19] I believe that this is what is happening in our hearts. When we have a greater hunger and thirst for the things of God, we receive more and more wisdom and understanding, and can stand in Truth.

---

[18] KJV
[19] KJV

CHAPTER 4

Angels on Assignment

Angels are active throughout the Old and New Testaments. We are told that angels guide and protect us as God's children. (Psalm 91:11, Exodus 23:20) They can appear in different forms and carry different assignments from the Lord. One way we often think of angels is as special messengers of God. The news that Mary was to give birth to the Messiah, the Savior of the world, was brought to her by an angel, Gabriel.[20] Earlier, an angel also appeared to Zacharias to say that his prayers had been heard and that he would also have a son.

> There appeared unto him an angel of the Lord standing on the right side of the altar of incense. And when Zacharias saw him, he was troubled, and fear fell upon him. But the

---

[20] Lk 1:26-38

angel said unto him, Fear not, Zacharias: for thy prayer is heard and thy wife Elizabeth shall bear thee a son, and thou shalt call his name John.[21]

When Mary visited Elizabeth's home, they embraced, and John the Baptist leaped within her womb. This Divine encounter was a strong witness confirming the angels' messages about both of their sons. The Scriptures speak of a great joy and gladness John brought to all, as he was filled with the Holy Ghost from his mother's womb.

> And many of the children of Israel shall he turn to the Lord their God. And he shall go before him in the spirit and power of Elias, to turn the hearts of the fathers to the children, and the disobedient to the wisdom of the just; to make ready a people prepared for the Lord.[22]

Angels also appear to people in dreams throughout Scripture, and we see an example in this same story. As we ponder how anyone can become More than a Conqueror, it should be plain as the nose on your face with

---

[21] Lk 1:11-13 (KJV)
[22] Lk 1:16-17 (KJV)

Mary and Joseph, this beautiful young Jewish couple, chosen by God to bring forth the Christ Child. When Mary shared that she was with child, you know Joseph had all kinds of thoughts running through his mind. *What, Mary? You are going to have a what? You are going to have a baby?* Our Father knew Joseph better than he knew himself, so in his surprised and bewildered mind, the Lord gave him a dream.

> But as he was thinking this over, behold an angel of the Lord appeared to him in a dream, saying "Joseph, descendant of David, do not be afraid to take Mary as your wife, for that which is conceived in her is of (from, out of) the Holy Spirit.[23]

There are many accounts in the Bible where God gave people dreams and night visions, and He still does this today. My Heavenly Father used dreams in my daddy's life in many different ways, and that gift of receiving dreams that are prophetic in nature was passed down to me, his baby daughter. Thank you, Lord Jesus!

Besides being sent to bring messages and speak through dreams, the Lord also gives angels other

---

[23] Mt 1:20 (AMPC)

assignments. An angel went before Abraham to help bring about God's plans for his life.

> The LORD, the God of heaven, Who took me from my father's house, from the land of my family and my birth, Who spoke to me and swore to me, saying, 'To your descendants I will give this land'—He will send His angel before you, and you will take a wife from there for my son.[24]

Also in Genesis, the Lord revealed to Jacob a vision of His army of angels. "And he dreamed that there was a ladder set up on the earth and the top of it reached to heaven; and the angels of God were ascending and descending on it!"[25] "Then Jacob went on his way and God's angels met him. When Jacob saw them, he said, "This is God's army."[26]

Jacob later spoke about an angel that brings redemption, calling it "The redeeming Angel [that is the Angel redeemer, not a created being but the Lord Himself] who has redeemed me continually from every evil."[27]

---

[24] Gn 24:7 (AMPC)
[25] Gn 28:12 (AMPC)
[26] Gn 32:1-2 (AMPC)
[27] Gn 48:16 (AMPC)

And in Psalms, we read that angels are also sent to guard and protect us. "The Angel of the Lord encamps around those who fear Him [who revere and worship Him with awe] and each of them He delivers."[28]

One of the reasons I have so loved (and still love) Psalm 34, and why I read and meditate on it so much, is that I battled lots of fear as a child. One of my biggest fears was that I didn't want my parents to reject me, especially my dad. He was always stern and firm and somewhat dominating. Knowing that my Heavenly Father sends angels to encamp around me brought me so much peace, and still does.

Finally, angels were sent to proclaim the resurrection of our Lord Jesus Christ:

> In the end of the Sabbath, as it began to dawn toward the first day of the week, came Mary Magdalene and the other Mary to see the sepulchre.
>
> And, behold, there was a great earthquake: for the angel of the Lord descended from heaven, and came and rolled back the stone from the door, and sat upon it.

---

[28] Ps 34:7 (AMPC)

His countenance was like lightning, and his raiment white as snow:

> And for fear of him the keepers did shake, and became as dead men.

> And the angel answered and said unto the women, Fear not ye: for I know that ye seek Jesus, which was crucified. He is not here: for he is risen, as he said.[29]

I pray that you, dear reader, would know that our Lord has placed angels in your life and in the life of your family. Bless the Lord, oh my soul and all that is within me — angels are active in our lives as Believers! They act on God's Word, and we activate the work of *angels in our midst by choosing to agree with God's Word.*

---

[29] Mt 28:1-6 (KJV)

CHAPTER 5

Perfect Timing

He gave His life to purchase freedom for everyone. This is the message God gave to the world at just the right time.[30] *I choose to believe that my Lord's timing is perfect in all things. Ecclesiastes tells us that "to everything there is a season."*[31] (Ecclesiastes 3:1), and Galatians speaks about timing as well, telling us "So let's not get tired of doing what is good. At just the right time we will reap a harvest of blessing if we don't give up.[32]

We must continue to stay in *faith* and *trust*, knowing that *God's timing is perfect*. We can run this race with the right mindset, determined to stay in God's Word daily, knowing that our Lord's timing isn't our timing. We can take heart in His faithfulness, having

---

[30] 1 Tm 2:6
[31] Eccl 3:1 (AMPC)
[32] Gal 6:9 (NLT)

confidence that our Lord makes a way when it seems there is no way.

When I first received the gift of the Holy Spirit, He spoke to me to *occupy*, which means to take possession, to engage, to take up a place or extend in place, or to take hold or control of enemy troops. He was faithful to speak to me about the call on my life, and in His timing He has helped me live in that calling. Dear reader, the Holy Spirit can also impress on your heart a word having to do with the call He has placed on you. Then the Holy Spirit will give you insight and wisdom about how to walk out that call.

I remember many years ago when my daddy was still alive on this side of eternity, the Holy Spirit spoke a word to me having to do with him personally. It was several years before He released me to give that word to my dad, him being an authority figure in my life and a great deal older — also very much an anointed man of God himself. I cried out to the Lord when the Holy Spirit finally spoke, "Now is the time for the Word I gave you, to share it with your dad. When you and Tom go to visit this weekend, ask Tom to take your mom to Sunday School and church, and you stay with your dad."

My father was in lots of pain in his knees and legs at that time, and sure enough he didn't make it to church. So my sweetheart husband agreed and took my mother to church while I stayed home with my dad. I was awakened in the wee hours of the morning and walked and prayed in the Holy Spirit for hours, speaking over this time I would have with Daddy. It was a beautiful, glorious time that we had, being alone together for several hours. We wept and laughed and had a wonderful time sharing, and I did a lot of praying for him. Tom and I arrived back home in Louisville, and Daddy called in a very joyous mood to tell me that since I was there preaching and praying he hadn't had any pain at all in his knees and legs. I told him that his Lord the Healer surely did His work on him through his baby daughter.

During these days my two younger brothers, Travis and Danny, had backslid. Daddy and Mother were praying diligently for their return to the Lord, and Daddy had always asked me to please pray for them as well. Both of them are enjoying Heaven now, although Travis left a lot of years before Danny.

I was five months pregnant with our youngest son, John Carlos, when I received a call at The Christian Beauty Salon. It was a Thursday or Friday and I was giving a comb out, had a couple of ladies under the dryer, and there was another client yet to be served. It was later in the day, as we hairdressers took some of our clients after they would get off from work at four or five o'clock and then travel thirty minutes or so to the salon.

The phone rang with the news that Travis had been shot in the mouth. When my husband and I arrived at Elizabethtown Hospital, my parents and siblings told me that since we had driven in from Louisville, we could visit Travis' room. He was unrecognizable; so very, very swollen, on oxygen and with tubes plugged in everywhere. What a sight to behold. My heart broke for him and also for his beautiful wife, Hallie Marie, and his two sweet daughters, Michelle and Joy.

Travis had several surgeries back to back and was in intensive care for a very lengthy time before he became conscious enough to recognize his family. He would put his hands together, a sign of "please pray for me." Travis was now convinced that his only hope was in Father God, Christ Jesus, and the glorious work of the Holy Spirit. He was a different man after coming through such trauma, even though he could not articulate it properly. Our whole family experienced the power of praying in faith, knowing that God's ear is open to our cries. In that small town of Leitchfield, Kentucky, everyone who heard about what happened to Travis and knew Christ Jesus as their Savior began to cry out to God for his soul and his healing. Without the prayers Travis prayed himself and that others prayed on his behalf, he would not have lived. God's timing in his life once again proved to be perfect. It was another lesson that as we wait for answers to our prayers, we can be convinced that God is building His character in us through the wait.

I am reminded of a particular Scripture that has been an amazing strength and encouragement over the years in my personal journey with God: "*[Jesus] told them* a parable to the effect that they *ought always to pray and not to turn coward (faint, lose heart, and give up).* [emphasis added][33]

All of us must learn the value of waiting. Waiting with expectation is a big part of what the Holy Spirit does within the Body of Christ Jesus. Our Father puts a promise in our hearts and we have the choice to rest in Him, knowing that His promises truly are *yes* and *Amen!*[34] His timing is never ours, so we must cast out the spirit of anxiousness, as anxiety is never our Father's desire for us. His plan is always *peace, peace, peace* in the midst of turmoil, knowing that this waiting is not in vain. Jesus is at work through the waiting process, bringing forth His image, likeness, and character in us so that we would continue seeking His Face. He wants for us a deep hunger and thirst for His living water, being convinced that He is working.

---

[33] Lk 18:1 (AMPC)
[34] 2 Cor 1:20

We should seek to wait without complaining or murmuring. This is not easy when the devil is working overtime trying to convince us that God's Word is not true. Oh, precious reader, but it is, it truly is! You may have to make the choice daily to believe that every promise in your Bible is yes and amen. You, as a true follower of the Lord Jesus Christ, are going to have to choose to wait with joy in your heart, soul, and mind, knowing that this time in your journey is bringing great and awesome benefits into your life and relationships.

> But they that wait upon the Lord shall renew
> their strength; they shall mount up with wings
> as eagles; they shall run, and not be weary;
> and they shall walk and not faint.[35]

This beautiful passage has been a glorious promise to me and carried me, keeping my soul and heart in an expectation of my Lord's great faithfulness.

There are many Scriptures showing the great benefits of waiting in victory, knowing that what you've been promised will surely manifest. Abraham had faith in a very long-awaited promise. He and Sarah had a twenty-five year wait for their child, Isaac. They had

---

[35] Is 40:31 (KJV)

first attempted to make the promise happen in their own strength. Sarah talked Abraham into marrying Hagar, saying perhaps they could have their promised child through her maid. That didn't work, because it was not God's plan. We have all had our Ishmaels. Our Father will not be manipulated. Our full dependency is to be on Him in faith, and we will inherit the promise.

The prophet Habakkuk speaks about waiting on God's promises. "This vision is for a future time. It describes the end, and will be fulfilled. If it seems slow in coming, wait patiently, for it will surely take place."[36] And later he says, "I have heard all about you, Lord. I am filled with awe by your amazing works. In this time of our deep need, help us again as you did in years gone by. And in your anger, remember your mercy.[37]

Knowing that we are on a journey of Faith, our trust in God's Word doesn't quit. Being convinced that God is His Word, we will not quit. Jesus taught His disciples that what is impossible with man is certainly not impossible with God[38]. So agree with God's promises. They are yes and amen!

---

[36] Hb 2:3 (NLT)
[37] Hb 3:2 (NLT)
[38] Lk 18:27

CHAPTER 6

Will You Obey Him?

If ye be willing and obedient ye shall eat the good of the land. (Isaiah 1:19 [KJV])

Obedience is better than sacrifice. (1 Samuel 15:22 [NLT])

Our Father is after our obedience. Read and reread, and read again out loud that this would be a glorious Holy Spirit revelation to your soul and heart.

This is what I told them: "*Obey me*, and I will be your God, and you will be my people. *Do everything as I say, and all will be well*![emphasis added][39]

---

[39] Jer 7:23 (NLT)

I remember even as a teenager having a healthy fear and awe of who my Savior the Lord Jesus Christ was because my Heavenly Father had truly blessed me with godly parents. Whether or not that is also your story, you can be confident that regardless of your parents' choices, you are very much called and chosen to be the Lord's hands and feet. He has set you apart to walk and live in your sphere of influence as *More than a Conqueror*, living in *His peace*.

> And I saw, and behold a white horse: and he that sat on him had a bow; and a crown was given unto him: and he went forth conquering, and to conquer.[40]

> No, despite all these things, overwhelming victory is ours through Christ, who loved us.[41]

Say it with me, "Bless the Lord, oh my soul and all that is within me." You have influence. You have an impact. There is an impartation coming from you, to your family first then then to those on the job and wherever else God places you.

---

[40] Rv 6:2 (KJV)
[41] Rom 8:37 (NLT)

In spite of your circumstances; you can be convinced that our Father uses any and all things in our lives to mold us into *His image and likeness*. Think about how children take on mannerisms like their earthly father. Choose, as the hymn says, to "Trust and obey for there's no other way."[42] We can place our confidence completely in the Lord. When we fully trust, we can do all things without fear. For those who struggle with fear, Joyce Meyer does have an amazing teaching on "Do it Afraid"[43].

My prayer for each one of us is that we trust fully in God's promises, knowing that our Lord stands by His Word to fulfill it in our lives. The beautiful old hymn, "Blessed Assurance" says it this way:

Blessed Assurance, Jesus is mine!

Oh, what a foretaste of glory divine!

Heir of salvation, purchase of God

Born of His Spirit, washed in His blood.[44]

---

[42] "Trust and Obey — Hymnology Archive." n.d. Hymnology Archive. https://www.hymnologyarchive.com/trust-and-obey.

[43] "Do it Afraid." n.d. https://joycemeyer.org/grow-your-faith/articles/do-it-afraid.

[44] "Blessed Assurance." n.d. https://www.hymnal.net/en/hymn/h/308.

Our choice to obey our Lord and Master impacts our lives greatly. Romans 6:16 says, "Don't you realize that you become *the slave of whatever you choose to obey*?[emphasis added]"[45]

Our struggle with obedience started at the very beginning with Adam and Eve in the Garden:

> Then Adam said, This [creature] is now bone of my bones and flesh of my flesh; she shall be called Woman, because she was taken out of a man. (Genesis 2:23 AMPC)

> And when the woman saw that the tree was good (suitable, pleasant) for food and that it was delightful to look at, and a tree to be desired in order to make one wise, she took of its fruit and ate; and she gave some to her husband, and he ate. (Genesis 3:6 AMPC)

These verses in the beginning of Genesis started the blame game that all of us have participated in. We blame our spouse for things, our parents, our older or younger siblings, a pastor, a teacher, or possibly a coach. Man's disobedience to Father God began in the Garden of Eden. God told them, "You guys can eat from all of this

---

[45] NLT

amazing, delicious fruit." But when Satan showed up with his big lie, Eve began to fall for the deception:

> And the woman said to the serpent, "We may eat the fruit from the trees of the garden, except the fruit from the tree which is in the middle of the garden. God has said, "You shall not eat of it.[46]

After both Adam and Eve ate of the forbidden fruit, Genesis 3 tells us, "Then the eyes of them both were opened, and they knew that they were naked; and they sewed fig leaves together and made themselves apronlike girdles."[47]

The Bible has many warnings for us about following God's plans and obeying his commands. In Leviticus 18:22, Moses says, "You shall not lie with a man as with a woman; it is an abomination."[48] And I Corinthians 6:9 tells us, "Do you not know that the unrighteous and the wrongdoers will not inherit or have any share in the Kingdom of God?"[49]

---

[46] Ge 3:2-3 (AMPC)
[47] Ge 3:7 (AMPC)
[48] AMPC
[49] AMPC

These are some very clear, strong statements that today's society needs to take heed to. "Do not be deceived (misled). Neither the impure and immoral, nor idolaters, nor adulterers, nor those who participate in homosexuality"[50] will inherit the Kingdom. The filth and the profanity and anything goes on television is darkness wanting to set up camp in our homes. But we are God's children of salt and light.

The goal that the Lord has for each of His children is that we deny our flesh and walk after the Holy Spirit. Our obedience to Him, in living a Christlike life, practicing loving our enemies, and doing good to others is so that we would be called the children of the Most High God. Laying our lives down and choosing who Jesus Christ truly is, we live and breathe and actually have our being. His Word tells us we are not our own. We are bought by His own blood.[51] We were born with a sin nature, but we are to heed the wooing of the Holy Spirit calling us to repent of our sins.

To repent is to have a change of mind. You can be a slave to sin, which leads to death, or you can choose to obey God, which leads to life. You are More than a Conqueror through your obedience to His Word. I want

---

[50] 1 Cor 6:9 (AMPC)
[51] 1 Cor 6:19-20

to share with you three P's that will greatly encourage you to know you are in Christ, being a doer of the Word and not just a hearer:

Knowing God's *Purpose* and receiving His *Power* that the Holy Spirit gives you through the gift of salvation and being baptized, not just in water but also in the glorious Holy Spirit, and receiving the *Passion* that Jesus came to give.

Truly it is this *Purpose*, *Power*, and *Passion* for Our King, the Lord Jesus Christ, that brings us to obedience and life in Him. Hebrews 11:6 says that Jesus is the rewarder of those that diligently seek Him. Still, it is our choice. Jesus taught His disciples that by their own words they are justified or condemned[52], so we must choose to obey or not to obey. Jesus did not say, "Hey guys, this journey in life will be a piece of cake." No, He told his disciples they would need to lay their lives down for the cause of the Kingdom.[53] He taught them to pray, "Thy Kingdom come, Thy Will be done on earth as it is in Heaven."[54]

In 2008, a special friend, Jo Ann Lofton, and I were praying in the Holy Spirit in the car on a beautiful late Fall evening. There was a glorious sunset, and the Holy

---

[52] Mt 12:37
[53] Mt 24:9
[54] Mt 6:10 (KJV)

Spirit in my belly spoke, *"Come up higher."* With that impression, I immediately thought of a passage in Revelation (John speaking):

> After this I looked, and behold, a door standing open in heaven! And the first voice which I had heard addressing me like [the calling of] a war trumpet said, "Come up here, and I will show you what must take place in the future."[55]

Our Father is calling us up to a higher realm in His Holy Presence. As we walk in obedience, we can be seated with Him in heavenly places. Colossians 3:1 tells us, "If ye then be risen with Christ, seek those things which are above where Christ sitteth on the right hand of God."[56]

---

[55] Rev 4:1 (AMPC)
[56] KJV

CHAPTER 7

Our Daily Bread

I can almost make a meal just by eating bread. Our Texas grandson, Pierce Thomas, is a lot the same way. We must have daily bread to live. God's Word speaks of the importance of bread throughout its pages, starting at the very beginning in Genesis, and continuing into the New Testament.

In the sweat of your face shall you eat bread until you return to the ground, for out of it you were taken. (Genesis 3:19 AMPC)

Eat it with bread made without yeast. For seven days the bread you eat must be made without yeast, as when you escaped from Egypt in such a hurry. Eat this bread — the bread of suffering — so that as long as you

> live you will remember the day you departed from Egypt. (Deuteronomy 16:3 NLT)

> Cast thy bread upon the waters for thou shalt find it after many days. (Ecclesiastes 11:1 KJV)

In the book of Ruth, in the first chapter, Ruth makes the choice to go with Naomi to return to the country of Moab; for Naomi had heard how the Lord had visited His people in giving them bread during the famine.[57] In 1 Kings, God commands the ravens to bring bread to Elisha.[58] And in the awesome book of Proverbs, Chapter 31 tells us all about the wise woman and that "she looketh well to the ways of her household, and eateth not the bread of idleness."[59]

I love what Moses says in Deuteronomy 8:3: "And He humbled thee and suffered thee to hunger, and fed thee with manna which thou knewest not, neither did thy fathers know; that he might make thee know that man doth not live by bread only, but by every word that proceedeth out of the mouth of the Lord doth man live."[60] Later, in Matthew 4, Jesus quotes this scripture when the devil was tempting Him in the desert.

---

[57] Ru 1:6
[58] 1 Kgs 17:4
[59] Prv 31:27 (KJV)
[60] KJV

Then was Jesus led up of the Spirit into the wilderness to be tempted of the devil. And when he had fasted forty days and forty nights, he was afterward an hungred. And when the tempter came to him, he said, If thou be the Son of God, command that these stones be made bread. But he answered and said, It is written, Man shall not live by bread alone, but by every word that proceedeth out of the mouth of God.[61]

In the New Testament, Jesus taught his disciples to remember him by breaking bread together:

The Lord Jesus the same night in which he was betrayed took bread: And when he had given thanks, he brake it, and said, Take, eat: this is my body, which is broken for you: this do in remembrance of me. After this manner also he took the cup. When he had supped, saying, this cup is the new testament in my blood: this do ye, as oft as ye drink it, in remembrance of me.[62]

---

[61] Mt 4:1-4 (KJV)
[62] 1 Cor 11:23-25 (KJV)

Our Bibles teach us to do this in remembrance of Christ's death and burial and His glorious resurrection. For He truly is alive in our hearts and seated in the heavens at the right hand of the Father.

On our wedding day, Tom and I took Holy Communion together, which was a beautiful moment. I also remember when my saintly mother was still on this earth, living in Kentucky. Every week I would visit her and I felt like the sweet Holy Spirit impressed on my heart to take Holy Communion with her. It was very dear to the both of us. And when our son, John Carlos, was attending Oral Roberts University, he came home for the weekend. Once again the Holy Spirit prompted me to have us, as a family, participate in Holy Communion before he left again. Oh, how special it was!

The practices of the Early Church continued with breaking bread together. Acts 2:42 says that "they continued steadfastly in the Apostles' doctrine and fellowship, and in breaking of bread, and in prayers."[63] Later in Acts, the Apostle Paul "took bread, and gave thanks to God in presence of them all: and when he had broken it, he began to eat."[64]

---

[63] KJV
[64] Acts 27:35 (KJV)

Perhaps the most beautiful New Testament Scripture about bread is what our Lord Jesus says about Himself:

> Our forefathers ate the manna in the wilderness; as the Scripture says, He gave them bread out of heaven to eat. Jesus then said to them, I assure you, most solemnly I tell you, Moses did not give you the Bread from heaven [what Moses gave you was not the Bread from heaven], but it is My Father Who gives you the true heavenly Bread. For the Bread of God is He Who comes down out of heaven and gives life to the world. Then they said to Him, Lord, give us this bread always (all the time)! Jesus replied, I am the Bread of Life. He who comes to Me will never be hungry.[65]

The Word of God teaches us that those who hunger and thirst for righteousness will be filled.[66]

Jesus is Bread. He doesn't just have bread to give us, *He is the Bread* that He gives us. He is the Bread of the Passover – unleavened, striped, pierced. He is the

---

[65] Jn 6:31-35 (AMPC)
[66] Mat 5:6 (NIV)

Bread of the tabernacle – made with fine flour. Bread of the assembly and Bread of the individual. He is the Bread of Bethlehem – sent from heaven. Given to all who receive. He is the Broken Bread – the Bread of Emmaus, the Bread of Melchizedek, the Bread of the wilderness.

One of the ways you can have a Holy Spirit atmosphere in your life is to play beautiful, anointed gospel music in your home or business. My dear special sister in Christ, Denice, was my roommate when we were missionaries in Southern India. We used cassette tapes to play anointed music or the Holy Scriptures. Gospel music can be such an encouragement in our lives as Believers. Before our sons left for college, there was a gospel song that was very popular. It says, "Keep casting your bread upon the waters."[67] The song is based on Ecclesiastes 1, and it has a great message about knowing that what you sow does return in our Lord's timing. We can trust our Heavenly Father with our daily bread, and our Lord Jesus says that He is our Bread of Life!

---

[67] "The Gaither Vocal Band – Bread Upon the Water." n.d. Genius. https://genius.com/The-gaither-vocal-band-bread-upon-the-water-lyrics.

CHAPTER 8

Set Your Minds

Set your minds and keep them set on what is above (the higher things), not on things that are on the earth. For [as far as this world is concerned] you have died and your [new, real] life is hidden with Christ in God. When Christ, who is our Life, appears, then you also will appear with Him in [the splendor of His] glory. (Colossians 3: 2-4 AMPC)

When our sons, Tom and John, were still home, I would share with them about how we are dead to sin and alive in God. The Bible speaks much about how important it is to fix our minds on Him:

Whatever is true, whatever is worthy of reverence and is honorable and seemly, whatever

is just, whatever is pure, whatever is lovely
and loveable, whatever is kind and winsome
and gracious, if there is any *virtue* and *excel-
lence*, if there is anything worthy of *praise*,
think on and *weigh* and take *account* of these
things [*fix your minds on them*].[emphasis
added][68]

Our Bibles tell us to "let this mind be in you which
was also in Christ Jesus."[69] The Word says that as a man
thinketh, so is he.[70] We are called to guard our minds
and hearts. Experts have proven that if you think on
something long enough, you will act that out. This is
why it is important to be mindful of your thought life.

When I look back on my childhood, I see that my
mother knew the secret of being thankful and staying
her heart and mind on what is lovely and lovable. She
so abounded in her love for Christ Jesus that she would
sing beautiful old hymns as she washed the dishes and
did other work around the farmhouse. Daddy also had
a gospel mindset at all times. He would often say, "The
more you serve the Lord and give yourself over to Him,
the more you want more of who He is." Daddy was quick

---

[68] Phil 4:8 (AMPC)
[69] Phil 2:5 (KJV)
[70] Prv 23:7 (KJV)

to witness to folks at work and everyone he came in contact with. The example that both my dad and mom set in living out their faith before their six children was remarkable. They truly showed and lived out the Fruit of the Spirit. The old church where Daddy gave his life to the Lord Jesus Christ was needing to be replaced so he and other men in the community built a new church called Bloomington General Baptist. That was where Mother and Daddy and their six children attended. We didn't have a pastor weekly; they came in around once a month.

Our family didn't have a large home, it was smaller than some of the other folks that attended our church, but anyone was always welcomed with much hospitality. It was my parents who would have the pastor spend Saturday night with us before he would preach the next morning. Our childhood friends also felt welcome, and enjoyed sharing meals with us. My parents' hospitality carried over to their children once we were grown and had our own homes.

I know now that it was Christ Jesus in my parents that caused them to be happy and generous and in love with our Father in Heaven. And although Mother felt more free to show her affection to Dad than he did with her, I also know that they were in love with each other.

I love to pass on what I learned from my parents and from other life circumstances about the importance of staying our minds and thoughts on Christ Jesus. Do you know your actions will follow your thoughts? Your soul is to be trained to act upon the word of God, and your body will obey the command of your mouth. It is of utmost importance that we as people be set apart as His workmanship created in Christ Jesus for good works.[71] Our Lord, Master, Healer, Deliverer, desires that we stay our thoughts on His great promises!

When I was about ten years old, my Great Aunt Mollie Moore was up in age, probably in her mid-eighties, living nearby in Millerstown, Kentucky. My mother, being her niece, was very concerned about her living alone, and she persuaded my daddy to bring her to live with us. Precious Aunt Mollie made an indelible impression on me, all for good. She had outlived three husbands and was healthy for her age. She had a large family Bible that she would lay in her lap and a magnifying glass with a long handle, and she would read her Bible in a rocking chair that she brought from her home. There were many times when we would be running around through the house and our dear Aunt Mollie would be bowed on her knees before her rocking chair.

Aunt Mollie lived with us for several years. When I was about 13 years old, she approached my parents and

---

[71] Eph 2:10

told them she wanted to purchase a Lane oak chest for me, so that I could begin to collect special household items such as sheets, pillow cases, nice linens, tablecloths, and beautiful dishes. My parents told her she didn't need to do that, but in her day that was how it had been done, and she was headstrong. I believe Aunt Mollie wanted to purchase that hope chest for me because I gave her more attention than my siblings did. My parents took her to a large mercantile store called the Big 7. It carried nice furniture, clothing, shoes of all styles and colors, and was also the largest grocery store in the town. I received an oak chest with a beautiful bright forest green lining.

One of my strongest memories of Aunt Mollie is that she would say to me often, "What is on your mind? What are you thinking about?" To you, my dear reader, I am asking the same question: What is on your mind? What is your thought life made up with? Have you, as a confessing believer, learned the value of taking every thought captive to the obedience of Christ Jesus Our Lord?[72] "For the weapons of our warfare are not carnal, but mighty through God to the pulling down of strong holds."[73]

---

[72] 1 Cor 10:5
[73] 1 Cor 10:4 (KJV)

I love the fact that godly choices have great benefits. The Psalmist, David, tells us "forget not" the benefits of serving the Lord.[74] There are many great rewards in choosing to have a made up mind that you will stay your thoughts on Him. Your Father finds great pleasure in His children who choose to remember who He is. I have purposefully used the word "choose" because on any given day you, the reader, have a choice about what your thoughts are going to be. Our Father wants our minds to be filled with wholesome thoughts of His great faithfulness. We speak God's Word that we have chosen to "have the mind of Christ."[75] We ask our divine Helper, the awesome Holy Spirit who has found His home in our hearts, that we, with our mind on Christ Jesus, can be the one to speak Life into people's lives. We should not be so preoccupied that we have no time for other people. Everyone in our lives is valuable to our Heavenly Father, and should be to us.

It is a beautiful and very helpful, healthy habit to start your day with your mind and heart on your Savior Jesus Christ. You will receive a renewed mind and soul as you make the choice to start your day with Him in your thoughts, and a desire to be led by the impressions

---

[74] Ps 103:2 (KJV)
[75] 1 Cor 2:16 (KJV)

of the Holy Spirit within you. Jesus told his disciples in John 14:6 "I am the Way, the Truth, and the Life."[76] One of our Lord's names is Truth. Do you want to know truth? Become a student of God's Word.

Our Father's desire is that we agree with His Word that we are victorious through and by the shed blood of the Lord Jesus Christ. Are you familiar with the old gospel song, "Power in the Blood"?[77] Or the hymn that declares, "What can wash away our sins? Nothing but the blood of Jesus."[78] There is no condemnation for those who belong to Christ Jesus. Do not allow the enemy to condemn you. Stand your ground in your Lord Jesus; we are in the Truth.

The Law of Moses was unable to save us because of the weakness of our sinful nature. Father God sent His only begotten son to die on a cruel cross so that we could live out of the new nature that we received when we were born again. The King James Version of the Bible says, "To be carnally minded is death; but to be spiritually minded is life and peace."[79] We must choose to stay our minds on obedience to Jesus Christ.

---

[76] AMPC

[77] "Would You Be Free From Your Burden of Sin." n.d. https://www.hymnal.net/en/hymn/h/1009.

[78] "What Can Wash Away My Sin." n.d. https://www.hymnal.net/en/hymn/h/1008.

[79] Rom 8:6

Our Lord tells us in His Word that He is the Prince of Peace[80] and He will lead us by His peace. The Holy Spirit that is in us through the new birth is our Counselor. He is our Instructor, our Teacher. Jesus said that his sheep "know [my] voice and a stranger will they not follow."[81] We choose to remind ourselves that the Holy Spirit in our hearts leads us by peace and joy. Our Lord never condemns us. He always leads us into truth.

I am reminded of Jeremiah 29:11, which says "'For I know the plans I have for you', says the Lord. 'They are plans for good and not for disaster, to give you a future and a hope'."[82] You can be confident that the enemy of all mankind wants us to think negative, fearful thoughts. We must be determined to fill our minds with good thoughts, thoughts of our Father's love and mercy, His great goodness, His great faithfulness. Our Bibles have much to say about our minds, our thoughts, our thinking. When we meditate on the greatness of our Lord and dwell on all His promises, we will have peace. You can't run out to the nearest drug store or grocery store and purchase peace of mind. You will have to make the decision, *I'm going to stay my mind on my Lord's promises.*

---

[80] Is 9:6
[81] Jn 10:4-5 (KJV)
[82] NLT

This is a great Scripture to memorize about the mind:

> Thou wilt keep him in perfect peace, whose mind is stayed on thee: because he trusteth in thee. (Isaiah 26:3 KJV)

We choose our thoughts. Read with me from Romans 12:

> I beseech you therefore, brethren, by the mercies of God, that ye present your bodies a living sacrifice, holy, acceptable unto God, which is your reasonable service. And be not conformed to this world: but be ye t transformed by the renewing of your mind, that ye may prove what is that good, and acceptable, and perfect, will of God.[83]

Later in this same chapter, we are reminded, "Be of the same mind one toward another. Mind not high things, but condescend to men of low estate. Be not wise in your own conceits."[84]

---

[83] Rom 12:1-2 (KJV)
[84] Rom 12:16 (KJV)

Your thought life will determine much of what you speak. If your thinking is in line with God's promises, you will speak them. Our Savior tells us that He is One with the Father. And if you have experienced receiving Jesus Christ as your own personal Savior, He is telling you that you are one with Him.[85] Be determined that with the help of the Holy Spirit you will have the mind of Christ to set the captive free from worry.

The books of Philippians and 1 Timothy have several amazing Scriptures about setting our minds:

> Only be sure as citizens so to conduct yourselves [that] your manner of life [will be] worthy of the good news, (the Gospel) of Christ, so that whether I [do] come and see you or am absent, I may hear this of you: that you are standing firm in united spirit and purpose, striving side by side and contending with a single mind for the faith of the glad tidings (the Gospel). (Philippians 1:27 AMPC)
>
> Fulfill ye my joy, that ye be likeminded, having the same love, being of one accord, of one mind. Let nothing be done through strife or vainglory; but in lowliness of mind let each

---

[85] Jn 14:20

esteem other better than themselves. Let this mind be in you: which was also in Christ Jesus. (Philippians 2:2-5 KJV)

If any man teach otherwise, and consent not to wholesome words, even the words of our Lord Jesus Christ, and to the doctrine which is according to godliness; He is proud, knowing nothing but doting about questions and strifes of words, whereof cometh envy, strife, railings, evil surmisings, Perverse disputings of men of corrupt minds and destitute of the truth, supposing that gain is godliness: from such withdraw thyself. But godliness with contentment is great gain. (1 Timothy 6:3-6 KJV)

For the love of money is the root of all evil: which while some coveted after, they have erred from the faith, and pierced themselves through with many sorrows. But thou, oh man of God, flee these things; and follow after righteousness, godliness, faith, love, patience, meekness. Fight the good fight of faith, lay hold on eternal life, whereunto thou art also called, and hast professed a good profession before many witnesses. (1 Timothy 6:10-12)

Don't you love that he called it "the *good* fight" and wrote "lay hold on eternal life"? When you choose to have the mind of Christ and sensitivity to the Holy Spirit, you will have healthy, wholesome thoughts.

> You will guard him and keep him in perfect and constant peace whose mind [both its inclination and its character] is stayed on You, because he commits himself to You, leans on You, and hopes confidently in You. So trust in the Lord (commit yourself to Him, lean on Him, hope confidently in Him) forever; for the Lord God is an everlasting Rock [The Rock of Ages].[86]

This scripture reminds me of the story of the author that penned the great hymn, "Rock of Ages".[87] On November 4, 1740, this baby in Farnham, England was given the name Augustus Montague Toplady. His father died in a war, he was spoiled by his mother, and his friends thought of him as a weak, sickly boy. Many

[86] Is 26:3-4 (AMPC)
[87] "Praise of the Week: Rock of Ages (1776)." St Stephen's Comely Bank Church. November 13, 2020. https://www.comelybankchurch.com/praise-of-the-week-rock-of-ages-1776/.

of his own relatives disliked him. But Augustus began to seek the Lord.

At eleven years old, Augustus wrote on his birthday, "I praise God I can remember no dreadful crime, to the Lord be the Glory." Shortly after, he was preaching sermons to whoever would listen. He was the same age as his Lord Jesus was when He went to the temple with his parents, Joseph and Mary, and read from Isaiah:

> The spirit of the Lord God is upon me. Because the Lord has anointed and qualified me to preach the Gospel of good things to the meek, the poor, and the afflicted; He has sent me to bind up and heal the brokenhearted, to proclaim liberty to the [physical and spiritual] captives and the opening of the prison and of the eyes to those who are bound.[88]

At fourteen, Augustus began writing hymns, and at sixteen received Christ as Savior during a barn service. God called him as an Anglican priest in his early 20s. Augustus was very opposed to John Wesley's Arminian theology and challenged him often in writing. A 1776 article written by Augustus spoke of God's forgiveness,

---

[88] Is 61:1 AMPC

and was meant to be a message against Wesley. At the end of the article was this poem:

Rock of Ages, cleft for me,

Let me hide myself in Thee!

Let the water and the blood,

from Thy riven side which flowed,

Be of sin the double cure:

save from wrath and make me pure.[89]

Each one of us could use this poem as a sincere prayer to our awesome Heavenly Father in Jesus' name.

Our Heavenly Father is after a heart that would love our enemies and do good to those who would despitefully use us.[90] It is interesting that Augustus Toplady and John Wesley were not so different after all. Wesley penned a beautiful hymn a few decades prior, which was very similar to "Rock of Ages," the title being "O Rock of Salvation."

O Rock of Salvation,

---

[89] Kerwin, Jim. 2019. "Rock of Ages | Finest of the Wheat." Finest of the Wheat. August 12, 2019. https://finestofthewheat.org/rock-of-ages/.
[90] Mat 5:44 (KJV)

Rock struck and cleft for me.

Let those two streams of Blood and Water

which gushed from thy side,

bring down pardon and holiness into my soul.[91]

Holiness is the end result of the good work of the Holy Spirit having his way in our hearts. Too often, even today, the Body of Jesus Christ decides to knit-pick our differences rather than celebrating our love for our King and our love for each other. I believe that if great unity will manifest in the Body of Jesus Christ, if we see Him in each other, the unsaved world will marvel at the love we have for one another and be drawn to our Savior.

Augustus died at a very young thirty-eight years old. His poem turned into a well-known and very loved hymn. His words give us much to set our minds on, and his life is a reminder to work for unity with other Believers.

All of us who want our lives to count for our Father's Holy Kingdom should live moment by moment

---

[91] Betjamin, John, Fred, RB 23.a.42, Mns, On the Lord's Supper, John Wesley, Lincoln - College, et al. 1747. "On the Lord's Supper." Second. Felix Farley. https://wesleyscholar.com/wp-content/uploads/2020/12/Hymns-on-Lords-Supper-2nd-ed-1747.pdf.

choosing to bring our thoughts and actions into obedience to Christ Jesus, our all-loving, all-giving, all-faithful Lord.

CHAPTER 9

Bearing Fruit and Having Abundant Life

God's Word calls us to be fruit bearing Christians. Jesus taught that we will know who is in Him by the fruit that they bear.[92] Let's explore what the Fruit of the Spirit is all about.

But the fruit of the [Holy] Spirit [the work which His presence within accomplishes] is *love*, *joy* (gladness), *peace*, *patience* (an even temper, forbearance), *kindness*, *goodness* (benevolence), *faithfulness*, *gentleness* (meekness, humility), *self-control* (self-restraint, continence). Against such things

---

[92] Mt 7:16

there is no law [that can bring a charge]. [emphasis added][93]

If we are confessing pure and true Christianity, God's Holy Spirit lives inside us, accomplishing these things. Love, joy, and gladness — people are drawn to those. Gentleness — I have so needed this very fruit, to be more gentle in all my relationships. Meekness, oh! Yes and amen to this fruit. I probably needed this fruit even more. I love what our Bibles say about Moses, that he was the meekest man on earth.[94] When I think about patience and long suffering, I remember how Christ Jesus our Lord is so patient with us. It is His will that we be patient and long suffering also with family and others in our lives

As we walk in the fruit of the Spirit, we live and move and have our being in Christ Jesus our Lord.[95] He has promised the Abundant Life for all of us who want who He is. John 10:10 says, "I came that they may have and enjoy life, and have it in abundance (to the full, till it overflows)."[96] This abundant life is yours for the taking!

---

[93] Gal 5:22-23 (AMPC)
[94] Nm 12:3
[95] Acts 17:28
[96] AMPC

There is no life outside of Christ, or of our Heavenly Father God. Genesis 2:7 tells us, "Then the Lord God formed the man from the dust of the ground. He breathed the breath of life into the man's nostrils and the man became a living person."[97] It is an amazing revelation how much our Heavenly Father, our Lord Jesus Christ, and the Holy Spirit as our Comforter and Instructor, give us life and lead us into our destiny.

Read with me Titus 2:14, which speaks about being zealous for the things of God:

> [He] gave Himself on our behalf that He might redeem us (purchase our freedom) from all iniquity and purify for Himself a people [to be peculiarly His own, people who are] eager and enthusiastic about [living a life that is good and filled with] beneficial deeds.[98]

When we realize that our sin nature has been resolved and conquered, we will be zealous for the things of God that produce life and bear good fruit, fruit that will last. Life can be a great challenge and a trial of our hope,

---

[97] NLT
[98] AMPC

trust, and faith daily. We must take up our cross and follow hard after our Glorious Abba Daddy, our King.

> My old self has been crucified with Christ. It is no longer I who live, but Christ lives in me. So I live in this earthly body by trusting in the Son of God who loved me and gave Himself for me.[99]

The abundant, fruit-bearing life comes when we remember we have been crucified with Christ because of His great love. It is now He who lives in us. Thank you, Lord Jesus!

---

[99] Gal 2:20 (NLT)

CHAPTER 10

Fast, Fasted, Fasting

Today I have given you the choice between life and death, between blessings and curses. Now I call on heaven and earth to witness the choice you make. Oh, that you would *choose life, so that you and your descendants might live*![emphasis added][100]

As called out, set apart children of the Most High God, we can believe and trust God to put an anointing on our lives to do *fasting* of some sort. I know I've touched on this in earlier chapters, but I believe it is close to the heart of our Heavenly Father. Jesus, our supreme example, practiced fasting and taught His disciples of its value. If you desire to do some fasting,

---

[100] Dt 30:19 (NLT)

ask the Holy Spirit what He would be saying to you personally.

> Is not this the fast that I have chosen? To loose the bands of wickedness, to undo the heavy burdens, and to let the oppressed go free, and that ye break every yoke? Is it not to deal thy bread to the hungry and that thou bring the poor that are cast out to thy house? When thou seest the naked, that thou cover him; and that thou hide not thyself from thy own flesh?[101]

> Sanctify ye a fast, call a solemn assembly, gather the elders and all the inhabitants of the land into the house of the Lord your God, and cry unto the Lord.[102]

He promised to hear us. We speak His Word in faith and confidence knowing that God's promises are yes and amen. We choose to be a two-edged sword!

Let's look at the story of when Jesus fasted:

> Then was Jesus led up of the Spirit into the wilderness to be tempted of the devil. And

---

[101] Is 58:6-7 (KJV)
[102] Jl 1:14 (KJV)

when he had fasted forty days and forty nights, he was afterward an hungred. And when the tempter came to him he said, If thou be the son of God, command that these stones be made bread.[103]

The enemy of all mankind knew full well that the Lord Jesus Christ was God incarnate, God the Father, God the Son, and God the Holy Spirit – three in One. The devil is such a liar, deceiver, and big coward that all he ever did is to be a copycat trying to mimic Christ. Jesus taught His disciples that the devil came to steal, kill and destroy and that He, our glorious Faithful Savior, came to give us life more abundantly. The devil told our King, after being on a forty-day fast, that He should turn stones into bread. But the very next verse says, "he answered and said, It is written, Man shall not live on bread alone, but by every word that proceedeth out of the mouth of God."

Jesus taught his disciples more on fasting when He was with them. Matthew 6:16-17 says, "Whenever you are fasting, do not look gloomy and sour and dreary like the hypocrites, for they put on a dismal countenance, that their fasting may be apparent to and seen by men.

---

[103] Mt 4:1-3 (KJV)

But when you fast, perfume your head and wash your face."[104] And later, in Matthew 9, the disciples of John the Baptist asked Jesus, "Why don't your disciples fast like we do and the Pharisees do?"[105] Our King of Kings answered, "Do wedding guests mourn while celebrating with the groom? Of course not. But someday the groom will be taken away from them, and then they will fast."[106]

Prayer and fasting is a wonderful gift to exercise. Pastor W. L. Rodgers and his son, Pastor Bob Rodgers, the Senior Pastor of Evangel World Prayer Center, have taught much about the value of giving yourself over to your Lord Christ Jesus in some type of fasting. There is sensitivity to the Holy Spirit in our hearts when we fast. Ivan Tait, the author of the book *Letters from God*, spoke many times at our church. I remember he once said, "God will honor you fasting a banana. It's not our fasting that our Father is after, it is our total obedience." No half-hearted commitment.

I was so very touched in my heart while visiting Louisville, Kentucky once, to attend Evangel World Prayer Center's 10:30 service. Pastor Bob Rodgers was sharing the burden he had for his son, Justin, and how

---

[104] AMPC
[105] Mt 9:14 (NLT)
[106] Mt. 9:15 (NLT)

he had fasted and prayed forty-four days for him. Our Father so honors our giving ourselves over to fasting. It is truly a supernatural anointing. I can report that today, Justin Rodgers is doing very well.

We should remember that fasting does not in any way change our Father. Fasting changes us. Many pastors and churches call a fast shortly after the beginning of the New Year. When you seek the Lord about the type of fast He has for you, your calling will look different than for others. Some folks cannot fast because of being on certain medications. Some drink only water, others drink juices. Some people fast from all desserts or coffee. I once heard Gloria Copeland say that the Lord asked her to fast from television. If we are following God's lead, fasting will be a healthy thing in our lives, similar to a detox. Our Father desires us to know His Plan and Purpose for our fasting, that we would find delight in being willing and obedient to the impressions of the Holy Spirit. I have had folks say to me, when there was a death or another kind of tragedy, that they would realize that they hadn't eaten in several days, and realized the Holy Spirit had worked that in their lives.

Let's look at another example in Scripture where God honored the prayers and fasting of His people, in the small book of Esther. A man named Haman had planned to destroy the Jewish people and convinced the king to give a decree that they would be killed. Here is what happened next:

> Now when Mordecai learned all that was done, [he] rent his clothes and put on sackcloth with ashes and went out into the midst of the city and cried with a loud and bitter cry.
>
> He came and stood before the king's gate, for no one might enter the king's gate clothed with sackcloth.
>
> And in every province wherever the king's commandment and his decree came, there was great mourning among the Jews, with fasting, weeping, and wailing, and many lay in sackcloth and ashes.[107]

Mordecai played a major part in saving the precious Jewish people. Next, we see Esther, the king's Hebrew wife, stepping into her part of God's plan.

> On the 3rd day [of the fast], Esther put on her royal robes and stood in the royal or inner court of the king's palace opposite his [throne

---

[107] Est 4:1-3 (AMPC)

room]. The king was sitting on his throne, facing the main entrance of the palace.

And when the king saw Esther the queen standing in the court, she obtained favor in his sight, and he held out to [her] the golden scepter that was in his hand. So Esther drew near and touched the tip of the scepter.

Then the king said to her, What will you have, Queen Esther? What is your request? It shall be given you, even to the half of the kingdom.[108]

It was prayer and fasting that eventually destroyed Haman's wicked plot to destroy God's chosen people. The king heard Esther's requests and not only stopped the evil plan, but ordered Haman's death.

Then the king Ahasuerus said to Queen Esther and to Mordecai the Jew, Behold, I have given Esther the house of Haman, and him they have hanged upon the gallows because he laid his hand upon the Jews.[109]

---

[108] Est 5:1-3 (AMPC)
[109] Est 8:7 (AMPC)

There is great power in fasting. When we deny our flesh, our spirit has an increase. One of the amazing things that the Lord has gotten my attention with through fasting is that I become very sensitive to the still voice of the Holy Spirit.

This is a very good time to seek the Lord about adding fasting to your prayers. And be sure that you seek our Heavenly Father through your fasting. Zechariah 7:5 says, "When you fasted and mourned in the fifth and seventh months, even those seventy years you were in exile, was it for Me that you fasted, for Me?"[110] Let your fasting be for Him, and see what the Holy Spirit will do in your life.

[110] AMPC

CHAPTER 11

Heal, Healed, Healing: The Healer in You

This chapter is dedicated to every reader who would be holding this book in their hand, or listening on a CD, or seeing this on Facebook, Twitter, or Instagram — however this word got to you.

I would first say to you that the God of the Holy Bible, the only true and living God, the God that lives and dwells in the heart of every Believer, has predestined you to have a revelation. No matter your creed, color or culture, the Lord God that sits in the Heavens this very moment tells *you personally* that you are more than a conqueror, an overcomer. You are undefeated. You are the delivered. You are the healed. You can have a made up mind that you are healed spiritually. No longer carrying stuff around like past wounds and hurts or offenses. Be determined to be free, and don't allow the enemy to replay negativity.

You are more than a conqueror. Be convinced and receive the revelation that God's Word works. God says that about His children who have received the shed blood of the Lord Jesus Christ. You have passed from darkness to Light, from being carnal (flesh) to being a vessel of honor whose thoughts and words bring great glory and magnification to your Heavenly Father. Bearing the fruit of the Spirit, we are healed from the inside when we receive the truth of God's Word in our souls.

When you, regardless of age or situation, give yourself unreservedly over to your King Jesus Christ and from your heart want His purpose for your life, there will be a transformation that takes place. When my Lord gives me divine appointments, I love to share with people that Jesus so loves them, and that He paid a horrendous price that they could walk free from emotional pain and physical pain.

Know deep in your soul, mind, will, and emotions that Jesus Christ is the Savior of the world, and that our Father that is seated in the Heavens did send the Healer — His Son, our Savior, to the earth with new hope. He waits patiently for His children to agree with His promises to all of us! You can be confident in the good work of salvation that He so gloriously and freely gave all mankind. As it says in Ephesians 2:8-9, "For by grace are ye saved through faith; and that not of yourselves: it is the gift of God: Not of works, lest any man should boast."[111]

You cannot put God in a box. He has many different ways to manifest healing in your life. You can have a two-fold heart healing. Many people have suffered from a broken heart. Other folks have had physical heart conditions that plague them. My saintly mother suffered from congestive heart failure, and my precious husband of my youth had to have stents put in his heart. The Lord can heal our physical, emotional, and spiritual hearts.

Our Father says in His word that man looks at the outer appearance, but He looks at people's hearts.[112] When He looks at you, does He see a person that has given Him your heart? Does He see a heart that desires to please Him; a heart that is truly willing and obedient; a heart that is convinced that Christ Jesus the Healer of all relationships, all diseases, all problems in His way in His timing.

All healing comes from God. Whether it comes through a doctor, a specialist, or home remedy, the healing comes through our Lord, the Great I AM. He spoke

---

[111] KJV
[112] 1 Sm 16:7

in Exodus 15:26, "I am the Lord who heals you."[113] Your Father has a longing in His heart for you to receive the revelation and understanding that *the stripes have been laid on His back for our healing*. He says that he heals the brokenhearted.[114] If you are suffering from a broken heart, you can receive your healing. When you give your brokenness to Him, the healing process starts. Jesus also says, "Come unto me, all ye that labor and are heavy laden, and I will give you rest."[115] That is also a form of healing.

Let's take a break and praise our Lord for being our awesome Healer. One of the first scriptures I ever memorized on healing was 1 Peter 2:24, "Who his own self bore our sins in his own body on the tree, that we, being dead to sins, should live unto righteousness: by whose stripes ye were healed."[116] In Psalm 30:2 King David spoke, "O Lord, my God, I cried unto thee, and thou hast healed me."[117] And in another beautiful word for all of us, David says, "He forgives all my sins and heals all my diseases."[118]

---

[113] NLT
[114] Psalm 147:3
[115] Mt 11:28 (KJV)
[116] KJV
[117] KJV
[118] Psalm 103:3 (NLT)

Our Father is in the healing business. He is the healer of marriages. He is the Healer of finances. When we choose to be willing and obedient to give when He prompts us to give of our finances and our tithes and prayers for those He has put in our lives, His Word promises that He will rebuke the devourer for our sakes.[119] Don't you love His promises? We choose to praise Him for His mighty acts.

I pray that you will believe and receive that your awesome Heavenly Father has provided healing for you. Ask Him if there is a hindrance to your healing. He will tell you if there is.

Our King, the Lord Jesus Christ, wore the crown of thorns so that we could have peace in our thought lives as well. I so appreciate Joyce Meyer's book on this subject, *The Battlefield of the Mind*. Our Lord wants to give us deliverance (being set free) from insecurities, inferiorities, and complexes. I was once self-righteous, prideful, religious, and carried all kinds of hang-ups. Our Heavenly Father chooses to look beyond all of our weaknesses and imperfections and see our hearts that desire the Fruit of the Spirit.

I had to be set free from a spirit of fear. Our Father tells us in 2 Timothy 1:7, "For God hath not given us

---

[119] Mal 3:11

91

the spirit of fear; but of power, and of love, and of a sound mind."[120] I also had to be set free from a spirit of religion and a very ugly spirit of pride. Our Bibles tell us that pride comes before the fall.[121] *How grateful I am that the Holy Spirit is faithful to continue working in us to set us free from any and all spirits that are unlike who Christ Jesus tells us we are. We are overcomers, more than conquerors, yielding and surrendering our will to the will of the Father.*

---

[120] KJV

[121] Prv 16:18

CHAPTER 12

Make the Choice to Rejoice

When I looked up in my New Living Translation dictionary/concordance the word "rejoice," the meaning was very interesting: *"Enjoy, Glad, Happy, Joy."* This should tell all of us that our awesome Heavenly Father's heart is that His children would enjoy being born again, knowing that *we have been washed in the soul cleansing power of the blood* of our King, Master, Healer, Deliverer, Way Maker, the Way, the Truth and the Life. He is the light of the word, and we who have passed from death to life are the salt of this earth.[122] One of the many uses of salt is that salt preserves. You stay salty when you live in His Word daily, filling your mind and heart with His promises.

---

[122] Mt 5:13

There are so many scripture references through-out the Old and New Testaments for the glorious word "rejoice". Our loving, gracious Heavenly Father makes it very clear that his desire for us is to have a glad rejoicing heart that we are His dwelling place. The Holy Spirit has found His home inside of our hearts. *We abide in Him and He abides in us.*[123]

We do not rejoice because everything is okay or perfect in our lives; goodness no! It is because we have His mercy. We have His goodness, His great faithfulness poured out in our lives. Do you remember that amazing old hymn, "Great Is Thy Faithfulness"? When I did research on this beautiful hymn, I found out that the author was Thomas Obadiah Chisholm[124]. He was born in my home state, the Bluegrass State of Kentucky, in a log cabin. At sixteen years of age he began teaching school, even though he did not have any advanced education. Thomas came to Christ at age twenty-seven under the ministry of evangelist H. C. Morrison. In 1923, he wrote a poem, "Great is Thy Faithfulness",

---

[123] Jn 15:4

[124] Brantley, Taylor, Don Chapman, and Don Chapman. 2023. "The Story Behind: Great Is Thy Faithfulness." Hymncharts. Com. June 1, 2023. https://www.hymncharts.com/2022/08/15/the-story-behind-great-is-thy-faithfulness/.

which became the beloved hymn. George Beverly Shea later sang this song at the Dr. Billy Graham crusades.

Thomas O. Chisholm went through many ups and downs in his life. His favorite Scripture was Lamentations 3:22-23, "His compassions fail not. They are new every morning."[125] Haven't you found that to be oh so true when we choose to rejoice? Deuteronomy 12:7 tells us, "And there ye shall eat before the Lord your God and ye shall rejoice in all that ye put Your hand unto, ye and your households, wherein the Lord thy God hath blessed thee."[126] And later in the same book it says, "For the Lord will again rejoice over thee for good, as he rejoiced over thy Fathers.*"[127]*

My youngest brother was probably the most tenderhearted of all six of us. Carlos Daniel was his name. We called him Danny or Dan. Danny was always a giver, very kind-hearted. He was born with dyslexia, which is when you see a word, and it appears backwards. So my sweet, kind, loving, tenderhearted youngest brother came out of the womb with this handicap. I have the fondest memories of Danny before he left for Heaven. We would have wonderful, heartwarming conversations on the phone telling each other about our

---

[125] KJV
[126] KJV
[127] Dt 30:9 (KJV)

precious grandchildren and their special accomplishments. Danny had an extremely thankful heart for his only daughter, Evelyn Darlene, and his Christian, hardworking, son-in-law, Johnny Bracther, the son of a full gospel pastor that left for Heaven rather early in life. Evelyn Darlene did very well in school, which pleased Danny and his wife very much.

After Tom and I moved to Houston, Danny and I became quite a bit closer. His wife, Evelyn, was very ill at the time and was pretty much bedridden. But Danny had a hunger and a thirst for God's Word, and I was so very ready to share all of God's wonderful promises with him at this time in his life. Despite his struggles throughout life, he was able to rejoice in the Lord.

If we are truly born again, our Father desires we be loving and kind, showing mercy and grace on the job or out shopping or wherever He has us. Are we being His salt and light to all who we would be in contact with. We never know what hurts and struggles people are going through and how we can show them the love of our Lord Jesus Christ. I am reminded of some of the godly choices that my parents made, being loving and kind to all. They didn't have to attend the same church we did or be a relative, my mother and daddy were truly lovers of God and lovers of people. They were quick to help in any way they could.

I remember when my oldest brother, Rudd, was about ten or twelve, he broke his leg. During that time wearing the cast and using a crutch, he decided he wanted to see our Uncle Herman, Mother's only brother, who lived in Whiteland, Indiana. Our Uncle Herman and Aunt Rosa and their two sons, Dale Eugene and Jerry Wayne, were very special relatives. So loving and kind at Christmas, they loaded each one of us children with very special gifts. My parents agreed to let Rudd take a bus out of Leitchfield, Kentucky to Whiteland, Indiana. This was so special to my brother when he was dealing with his broken leg.

My mother was a real prayer warrior. Dad too, and he was obedient and willing to the call of God on his life to preach the gospel. So was my brother, Rudd. They stayed in faith and freely trusted God when my sister, Peggy, was diagnosed with a partial lung disease. In time, she was healed. Life presents storms and my parents had their share of them. They remained faithful to stay in church, stay filling themselves up with the Word of God, and stay in daily prayer. I will be forever grateful for this Christlike example.

Your Father is able to perform miracles in your life, regardless of your circumstances. He is "able to do exceeding abundantly above all that we ask or think, according to the power that worketh in us."[128] It is God's good pleasure to make this particular Scripture a reality in your life. When you gave your life to the Lord Jesus, all that He is He put inside of you.

Years ago, a friend of mine came to our home and spoke with me through the Glorious Holy Spirit that I was being called to a twenty-one day fast. My dear husband thought there was no way. But the Way Maker, the Lord Jesus Christ's, presence was alive in me and I didn't eat. (Well, maybe a couple of pretzels.) This was truly supernatural, the work of the Holy Spirit. Our sons were both still living at home, so I would bake a ham and all the trimmings. Tom and the boys ate well, and I would take the phone off the hook and sit at the table with them, sipping on tea or juice.

Don't allow the Thief, the Murderer, the Destroyer to get you thinking, "I have prayed so long and nothing has changed." Oh, there have been changes, even if they are not visible yet. It is truly our Father's delight to answer our prayers prayed in faith. In 1 Samuel, we read about Hannah's story of waiting for God's answered prayer. The Lord answered her, and Hannah said, "My heart rejoices in the Lord. The Lord has made

---

[128] Eph 3:20 (KJV)

me strong. Now I have an answer for my enemies; I rejoice because you rescued me."[129]

Live in the promises that God has made to you. All that any of us will ever receive from our Lord comes through exercising the faith that He has put in us. He said that the just live by faith[130], and *we are* the just through His shed blood. Take time to ponder and meditate on the price that your Savior paid. It was so we could live in faith, peace, and joy, having a supernatural rest in our souls. Not because all is perfect in our lives, but because He lives in us. The Life giver has found His home in the innermost part of our being. Our Lord inhabits our praises (Psalm 22:3), and the Holy Spirit is our guide, instructor, teacher, comforter, and peace. It is our turn to rejoice over His great gift of salvation to us.

---

[129] 1 Sm 2:1 (NLT)
[130] Hb 2:4

CHAPTER 13

Our Hearts

John 14:1 was definitely my daddy's favorite Bible verse. He quoted it very often, and not just when he was preaching. Our soon-coming King said to His disciples,"Let not your heart be troubled: ye believe in God, believe also in me."[131] In the same chapter He told them, "Peace I leave with you, my peace I give unto you: not as the world giveth, give I unto you. Let not your heart be troubled, neither let it be afraid."[132] And in Philippians 4:7, Paul writes, "And the peace of God, which passeth all understanding, shall keep your hearts and minds through Christ Jesus."[133]

Do you desire peace of mind and heart? These Scriptures I've shared with you tell you how to have it. The

---

[131] KJV
[132] John 14:27 (KJV)
[133] KJV

Bible has so much to say about our hearts. Many precious folks are carrying a broken heart. Jesus is speaking to you this very moment through the words of this book:

> The Spirit of the Lord is upon me, because he hath anointed me to preach the gospel to the poor; he hath sent me to heal the brokenhearted.[134]

Receive and believe that Christ Jesus has healed your broken heart. Believe with your heart that it has been healed. Open your mouth in faith, believing and saying, "Thank you, Lord Jesus, that You have healed me. I walk free with a new purpose for my life. Thank you, my Savior, for being the God of my healed heart and that you have new beginnings for me. Glory to your name."

There are those who are fainthearted, and the Scripture that comes to mind is this: "Let the weak say, I am strong."[135] You are not in denial when you say this. You are giving voice to your faith. You are justified by faith.[136] Our Father has paid for every heart to be free in His Son, who bore all our sins on the Cross.

---

[134] Luke 4:18 (KJV)
[135] Joel 3:10 (KJV)
[136] Romans 5:1

When Solomon succeeded his father, King David, for the throne, he asked God to give him "a discerning heart."[137] He asked for this because he wanted an understanding heart to judge the people. This request from Solomon pleased His Lord, because he did not ask for a long life or riches or his enemies' destruction, and God said "Behold, I have done according to thy words: Lo, I have given thee a wise and an understanding heart."[138]

Our Bibles speak to us not to harden our hearts by ignoring the wooing of the Holy Spirit. He desires to lead us in paths of righteousness, and we are to guard our hearts. Mirriam-Webster says that to guard means "to protect from danger, especially by watchful attention; to watch over; to tend to carefully."[139] We guard our hearts by keeping the truths of God's Word in our minds and heart. Joshua 22:5 puts it like this:

> But be very careful to keep the commandment and the law that Moses the servant of the Lord gave you: to love the Lord your God, to walk in obedience to him, to keep his

---

[137] 1 Kgs 3:9

[138] 1 Kgs 3:12 (KJV)

[139] "Guard." 2024. In *Merriam-Webster Dictionary*. https://www.merriam-webster.com/dictionary/guard#dictionary-entry-2.

commands, to hold fast to Him and to serve
Him with all your heart and all your soul.[140]

Out of the abundance of your heart your mouth will
speak. You can know what is in your heart by what is
coming out of your mouth. Ask yourself a simple question, "What am I speaking?" Are you often saying, "He
(or she) is driving me crazy!" Take a break and listen
to yourself. It doesn't take any effort to speak about our
circumstances. But we must choose to declare and decree
with faith in our hearts and minds to agree with God's
Word.

Psalm 7:9-10 says, "Bring to an end the violence of
the wicked and make the righteous secure —you, the
righteous God who probes minds and hearts. My shield
is God Most High, who saves the upright in heart."[141]
Can you say in hope and faith, "I have an upright heart,
and because of the condition of my heart, my shield is
my Lord."? God looks deep within the mind and heart.
We need to be conscious of the fact that nothing is hidden from the Lord. This can be either terrifying or com-
forting. Our thoughts have always been an open book

---

[140] New International Version
[141] NIV

to Him. You (we) can be confident that our Lord knows our motives.

One of the secrets of a close relationship with our Lord is to do as King David did: ask Him to search your heart. He knows our hearts. It is His desire that we know whether or not our intentions and motives are from a pure heart before Him. In the morning our minds are freer from problems, and we can commit the whole day to our Father. It will be a very great blessing to you personally if you awaken each morning and give Him your day; have that special time and peace to love on your Lord, read His promises, and make them very personal.

I recall viewing Dr. Billy Graham's funeral. One of his daughters shared about her mother's heart for the Holy Scriptures and how she would put her name in those Bible verses she would read. This thrills the heart of our Lord when we take His words into our hearts and souls. Jesus taught His disciples to say in the Lord's Prayer, "Give us today our daily bread."[142] No matter how great and amazing yesterday's devotion time was, we must have fresh bread for today. Please try starting your day with a special time to meet with your Father, with Bible in hand and a notebook or journal, and don't do all the talking. We can be still and know He is God.

---

[142] Mt 6:11 NIV

Deuteronomy 10:12-13 is a call to love and obedience:

> And now Israel, what does the Lord your God require of you? He requires only that you fear the Lord your God, and live in a way that pleases him, and love him and serve him with all your heart and soul. And you must always obey the Lord's commands and decrees that I am giving you today for your own good.[143]

I pray and believe that you will have a fresh enlightenment that loving God with all of your heart and soul has great benefits — more probably than any of us can grasp.

Moses continually spoke to the Israelites about the Lord and His awesome goodness and great faithfulness. Deuteronomy 10:17 tells us, "For the Lord your God is the God of gods and Lord of lords. He is the great God, the mighty and awesome God who shows no partiality and cannot be bribed."[144] Our heavenly Father is a God of justice. He has such awesome power that people cannot stand before Him without His mercy. Thank you, Lord, that your mercy is unlimited. When we receive a

---

[143] NLT
[144] NLT

revelation of His mercy toward all of us, we see what true love is, and how deeply God unconditionally loves us.

What is the deepest cry of your heart? Is it for a mended relationship with your child, parent, spouse, pastor, neighbor, or boss? There is danger in carrying an offense. I believe the solution is choosing to be a forgiver, not in word only but from our hearts. I heard the well-known teacher, Marilyn Hickey, speak once about how she forgave a woman in her church in faith. So we, from our hearts, can make the choice to forgive those who have wounded, hurt, betrayed, or abandoned us. Your Savior, the Lord Jesus, is reaching out to you with pleading arms, saying, *Come to me, you who would be heavy-laden, I have rest, supernatural rest, not of this world. This rest is from Me, your Savior, Lord, and Master; King of all kings. It is my delight to set your heart and soul free from all offenses, all turmoil, all anxiety.*

When you make a heart choice to be a forgiver, specifically naming what you are forgiving someone for and committing them to your Savior, then the Holy Spirit will start to work on their heart and soul. Just be sure to remind yourself that we are on a faith journey.

I remember all those many years ago when our sons were still very small children, I was racing out the door one day to be at Jan Ann's Beauty Salon. I whispered a sincere prayer, "Lord, give me a Scripture." Then I ran to my Bible, and my eyes fell on 2 Corinthians 5:7, "For we walk by faith, not by sight."[145] I have held on to that very Scripture to continually remind myself that when we go after God's heart and truly want His plan and purpose for our lives, not our way but His way, and when we eat the daily bread of His Word daily, there will be joy in our hearts.

Don't you just love it when your Lord causes your eyes to fall on the words of our Lord Jesus? The Bible is God's love letter, full of glorious, amazing promises to us. Our Father desires intimacy with His children. That's why I prefer Bibles that have what Jesus spoke in the color red. I deeply appreciate all the prophets of old and what they spoke, and the teachings of the Apostles Paul and Peter in all of their dear letters, and the promises that John wrote, as well as Matthew, Mark and Luke. But I love even more so what Jesus spoke in these books.

What an awesome blessing would be manifested, poured out on us as the Body of Christ, if we would choose to meditate on these tremendous words from the mouth of our Lord Jesus Christ in Luke 6:45:

> A good man out of the good treasure of his
> heart bringeth forth that which is good; and

---

[145] KJV

an evil man out of the evil treasure of his heart bringeth forth that which is evil; for of the abundance of the heart his mouth speaketh.[146]

Jesus has told us that we are going to have what we speak.[147] Charles Capps, a very anointed man of God out of Arkansas, penned a small booklet in 1976 entitled *The Tongue: A Creative Force* that has sold millions and millions of copies. My prayer for you is that you would make it a priority to purchase and read it, because you will certainly be blessed.

Let's remember the words of Moses to the Israelites in Deuteronomy 8:

And thou shalt remember all the ways which the Lord thy God had led thee these forty years in the wilderness, to humble thee, and to prove thee, to know what was in thine heart, whether thou wouldest keep his commandments, or no.[148]

---

[146] KJV
[147] Mark 11:24
[148] Dt 8:2 (KJV)

Please, special one, ask yourself what exactly is in your heart today and what you are speaking. Let's pray the Lord's Prayer together:

> *Our Father in Heaven*
> *may your name be kept holy.*
> *May your Kingdom come soon.*
> *May your will be done on earth*
> *as it is in heaven.*
> *Give us today the food we need,*
> *and forgive us our sins,*
> *as we have forgiven those who sin against us.*
> *And don't let us yield to temptation,*
> *but rescue us from the evil one.*[149]

You are privileged to choose to be a lover of God, to love all mankind, and to have a grateful, thankful heart.

---

[149] Mt 6:9-13 (NLT)

CHAPTER 14

Seek His Kingdom

Seek ye first the Kingdom of God, and His righteousness; and all these things shall be added unto you. (Matthew 6:33 KJV)

Moses, a great leader to the Israelites, continually tried to convince them that obedience has rewards and that being stiff-necked has consequences that are never good. Our carnal, or flesh, man is never what our Father intended for our journey with the Lord. To be carnally minded is death. To be spiritually minded is Life.

So be careful not to break the covenant that your God has made with you. Do not make idols of any shape or form, for the Lord, your

God has forbidden this. The Lord your God is
a devouring fire; he is a jealous God.

In the future, when you have children and grandchildren and have lived in the land a long time, do not
corrupt yourselves by making idols of any kind. This is
evil in the sight of the Lord your God and will arouse
His anger.[150]

This is a strong warning that God gave Moses for
His people. Make the choice to be a seeker of the honorable plan that He has for all His children. I want to
reiterate Matthew 6:33 again: seek the Kingdom of God
above all else and live righteously, and He will give you
everything you need.

In Psalm 10, King David says, "The wicked, through
the pride of his countenance, will not seek after God:
God is not in all his thoughts."[151] And in the same chapter, "His mouth is full of cursing and deceit and fraud:
under his tongue is mischief and vanity."[152] Later, David
tells God in Psalm 27:8, "When thou saidst 'Seek ye
my face; my heart said unto thee, thy face, Lord, will I

---

[150] Dt 4:23-25 (NLT)
[151] Ps 10:4 (KJV)
[152] Ps 10:7 (KJV)

seek."[153] And in Psalm 34:14 he says,"Depart from evil, and do good; seek peace, and pursue it."[154]

I love this translation of seeking God's heart and mind for His will and purpose for our lives: "O God, you are my God; I earnestly search [seek] for you. My soul thirsts for you; my whole body longs for you in this parched and weary land where there is no water."[155]

I also love these verses from Amos 5:

> For thus saith the LORD unto the house of Israel, Seek ye me, and ye shall live.[156]

> Seek him that maketh the seven stars and Orion, and turneth the shadow of death into the morning, and maketh the day dark with night: that calleth for the waters of the sea, and poureth them out upon the face of the earth: The LORD is his name.[157]

The earth is the Lord's and the fullness of things.[158] It is our Father's good pleasure that we fully enjoy the

---

[153] KJV
[154] KJV
[155] Ps 63:1 (NLT)
[156] Am 5:4 (KJV)
[157] Am 5:8 (KJV)
[158] Psalm 24:1

beautiful mountains and the oceans; that we find pleasure in vegetable gardens, flower gardens, the lavender fields in Utah and other places. When we seek our Father God, and He is our all in all, we do enjoy life in its fullness.

A great promise comes to us out of Matthew 7:7 for those who are seekers of our Lord: Seek and you will find! Dear heart reader, are you seeking the Lord Jesus for His purpose in the remainder of your days? You may possibly be very young, or maybe you have had many birthdays. What matters is, are you being salt and light? That's why we were all born — to be His vessel of honor and to bring Him glory!

Our lifetime goal should be to make Him famous, to point everyone in our lives to the Lamb of God who was slain, who spilled His life's blood that whosoever would receive the sacrifice He made could pass from death to life.

And isn't it wonderful to know that our Lord also seeks *us*? Luke 19:10 tells us, "For the Son of man is come to seek and to save that which was lost."[159] And in the beautiful parable of the lost sheep, Jesus says, "If a man has a hundred sheep and one of them wanders away, what will he do? Won't he leave the ninety-nine

---

[159] KJV

others on the hills and go out to search for the one that is lost?"[160]

Proverbs 8:17 says, "I love them that love me; and those that seek me early shall find me."[161] Seek Him every day, and you will know Him more!

---

[160] Mt 18:12 (NLT)
[161] Prv 8:17 (KJV)

CHAPTER 15

Humility

(Now Moses was very humble — more humble than any other person on earth.)

So immediately the LORD called to Moses, Aaron, and Miriam and said, "Go out to the Tabernacle, all three of you!" So the three of them went to the Tabernacle. Then the Lord descended in the pillar of cloud. (Numbers 12:3-5 NLT)

M oses found favor with God because of his humility. Let us ask ourselves, are we of a humble spirit? Are we wearing the coat of humility? Do we have a servant's heart? Our supreme example, our Lord Jesus Christ, humbled Himself and chose to wash His disciples' feet. How beautiful it is that the King of all

Kings, the God of Glory, would bow His knees and gird Himself with a towel and hold their dusty, dirty feet. (They wore sandals in Jesus' day.) In His amazing humility He even prepared a meal for His disciples and then let them come and dine with Him. He prepared fresh fish. Now the Bible doesn't tell us whether it was whitefish, swordfish, redfish, or tilapia, but isn't this an amazing scene of our Healer, Deliverer, Way Maker, the Truth, and the Life serving His disciples? Are you willing to serve also, starting with your family and then your friends and neighbors? Think of acts of kindness you can do from your heart.

I pray that each of us would be reminded of our Lord's great goodness, His amazing faithfulness. When we humble ourselves before Him, regardless of the task laid before us, we are continually called to return good for evil. When we choose to be humble in situations and circumstances where our flesh man wants to act up and act out, we literally gain new strength for this journey in life.

Psalm 138:6 says, "Though the Lord is great, He cares for the humble."[162] In the beautiful book of the Psalms, we can receive much comfort, wisdom, and everyday lessons. Most of them are prayers, and most

---

[162] NLT

of the prayers include praise to God. When we choose to be lowly of mind and humble of heart, considering all that God has done and is doing for us, His will for us becomes clear.

As my dear, close friend and glorious prayer partner, Jo Ann Lofton, often says, it is effortless — the Christ-like nature that the Holy Spirit puts inside us at the time of the new birth. His nature is loving forgiveness, pure and patient. Have we been quick enough to give heartfelt praise to our loving, forgiving, merciful, and gracious Father for His great faithfulness to us and our families? Are you aware that the God of the heavens and the earth delights Himself in you? Please do yourself a real favor and read and reread over and over Psalm 149:4: "For the Lord delights in his people. He crowns the humble with victory."[163]

Our soon coming King Jesus was spoken of by Zechariah, who said, "Rejoice, O people of Zion! Shout in triumph, O people of Jerusalem! Look, your King is coming to you. He is righteous and victorious, yet he is humble, riding on a donkey."[164]

The purpose of this book is to convince you, the reader, that regardless of what you are facing or walking

---

[163] NLT
[164] Zec 9:9 (NLT)

through, you can receive from your humble Savior, the Lord Jesus Christ, that you are His prized possession. He is very much in love with you.

The Apostle Paul's most important credential was that he was an eyewitness of the risen Christ.[165] The other Apostles had seen Christ in the flesh, but Paul was the next generation of believers. Still, Christ appeared to him. Paul was a zealous Pharisee, and had been an enemy of the Christian church — even to the point of capturing and persecuting believers.[166] Thus he felt unworthy to be called an apostle of Christ.[167] Though undoubtedly the most influential of the apostles, Paul was deeply humble. He knew that he had worked hard and accomplished much, but only because God had poured kindness and grace upon him.[168]

True humility is not convincing yourself that you are worthless, but recognizing God's work in you. As Jesus' disciples of this day, we are called to not only humble ourselves before our Lord Jesus Christ, but to be a humble spirit before all mankind. This means the stranger, the cashier who appears to be somewhat weary with her or his situation, and anyone else you encounter. You can

---

[165] Acts 9:3-6
[166] Acts 9:1-3
[167] 1 Cor 15:9
[168] 1 Cor 15:10

be that one to give them a sincere compliment. Believe me when I write to you that I have lived out trusting my Father in this. Before I leave our Texas home, I ask my Lord in faith to let me be a blessing. I say, "Father give me a word to bring encouragement, fresh hope and increase of faith." Many beautiful things have happened at places like Kroger, or department stores.

I was in the nearby Academy one day getting in a walk, since it was a pretty messy day here in Cypress, Texas, rainy and windy. I felt the light of God's Holy Presence moving in on me when I caught a glimpse of this beautiful gal. (I will call her Lisa.) I just immediately spoke, "You are a Believer, aren't you?" She responded, "Oh yes, I certainly am!" We had a beautiful time sharing the greatness of our heavenly Father together.

Some of God's children have believed the lie that they aren't really equipped to be a witness to anyone. "They probably would laugh at me", they might say. That has not happened to me and I have always been very vocal about my faith. We have a glorious Savior and Lord, and truly He is more than enough. Your Father has made you in His own likeness and image. He created us to be enough.

The Creator of the heavens and the earth made you very unique, meaning the only one. Our Father confirms that in the way that there are no two fingerprints the same out of the billions of folks inhabiting this earth. Your life has great purpose. You are valuable to your family. They so need your love and support, and especially your prayers.

Jesus taught His disciples, and He is still speaking to us, an important message in Luke 14:1. "For those who exalt themselves will be humbled, and those who humble themselves will be exalted."[169]

I am reminded of Dr. Billy Graham, his wife, Ruth, and their children. What a beautiful example of humility. He became so very admired, respected, and honored in every arena of life, yet he and his family remained very humble. All of their children love, honor, and serve the Lord Jesus Christ. Their daughter, Anne Graham Lotz, is an outstanding teacher and powerfully anointed preacher and author.

Writer Roy Lessin says that those who walk before God in humility are:

Weak enough to lean upon His strength

Small enough to look upon His greatness

Patient enough to draw upon His fullness

Poor enough to depend on His riches

Needy enough to count upon His grace[170]

---

[169] NLT

[170] Lessin, Roy. 2017. "Surrounded." *Dayspring* (blog). March 15, 2017. https://www.dayspring.com/articles/surrounded.

I choose to be lowly of mind and humble of heart. I choose to humble myself and to take on a servant's heart. I dwell in the secret place of the Most High God under the shadow of the Almighty. The Lord says that the meek "shall inherit the earth."[171] Humility — oh my, I have so needed this attribute in my life.

What does it mean to be more than a conqueror? It means that you have been humble enough to receive the truth about who your Heavenly Father is and who He says you are in Him. I recently heard the teacher, Joyce Meyer, speak about how we cannot please our Father and be obedient to His plan if we don't know His Word. In humility, seek Him through His Word and trust Him to let you be a blessing to others.

---

[171] Mt 5:5 (KJV)

CHAPTER 16

Our Words

The words we speak have a greater effect on our lives than we often realize or understand. Our Lord Jesus tells us in Matthew 12, "But I say unto you, that every idle word that men shall speak, they shall give account thereof in the day of judgment. For by thy words thou shalt be justified and by thy words thou shalt be condemned."[172]

Are we receiving the revelation that our words must be in line with our Father's words to receive what He has already provided for all of us? You will believe your own words about yourself more than the words I would speak to you. For instance, I can tell you "By His stripes you are healed,"[173] but nothing changes until you receive a revelation that our Lord's Word works. The

---

[172] Mt 12:36-37 (KJV)
[173] Is 53:5

gift of salvation is ours through believing in our hearts and speaking that you have given your heart to the Lord Jesus Christ. That's when salvation is yours. As it says in Romans,

> "If you declare with your mouth, 'Jesus is Lord' and believe in your heart that God raised Him from the dead, you will be saved. For it is with your heart that you believe and are justified, and it is with your mouth that you profess your faith and are saved."[174]

Are we speaking God's promises about our spouses, speaking the Word of the Lord about our children, speaking our faith about any and all situations in our lives? Stop now and give thought to what you are saying about your circumstances. The scripture that comes to my mind is, "Whosoever shall say unto this mountain, Be thou removed, and be thou cast into the sea; and shall not doubt in his heart, but shall believe that those things which he saith shall come to pass; he shall have whatsoever he saith."[175]

---

[174] Romans 10:9-10 (NIV)
[175] Mk 11:23 (KJV)

You may have to say what the Word says and what you are believing for some time.

There is the catch. It takes discipline and the glorious work of the Holy Spirit for us to continually declare and agree with the Word of the Lord when situations and circumstances seem the opposite. We have to make the decision to speak the Word and believe that His promises are yes and amen. He is bringing forth His fruit of love, joy, peace, long-suffering, gentleness, goodness, and faith. And in all of this, we are called to love our enemies, to do good to those who would despitefully use us.[176]

Those who belong to Christ Jesus have nailed the passions and desires of their sinful nature to the cross and crucified them there.[177] Daily giving ourselves over, we can speak out loud, "Holy Spirit, I give you control. I choose to be willing and obedient to the impressions of your voice within me." It is His desire to lead us; to instruct and guide us and that in all our ways we would acknowledge Him.[178] Take on a fresh determination to be led by the Holy Spirit in you. When we received Jesus Christ as our Savior, He put in us a new nature.

---

[176] Mt 5:44
[177] Galatians 5:24
[178] Prv 3:6

We yield to our new nature, and know that God's love in us never fails.[179]

What are you giving voice to today? Say with me, "I am more than a conqueror through Him that loved me." Agree with what He spoke about you. Are you believing in your heart the words of our great I AM that you are going to have what you say? Our words have importance and consequences. Researchers estimate that we make over 35,000 choices every day.[180] Because of that, let us give ourselves over to the leading of the Holy Spirit.

Are you saying about yourself what the Word of God says about you being more than a conqueror? That you can do all things through Christ who strengthens you?[181] Do you declare and decree the Word of God for your spouse, for your children, and grandchildren. Oh, yes!

My friend Sue Maybry, at about 85 or so, was an amazing prayer warrior. I believe she was a prophet. When I would pray for our grandchildren she would always remind me, "Carlene, and the great grandchildren." My very special friend and sister in Christ, Jo

---

[179] 1 Cor 13:8
[180] Hoomans, Joel. n.d. "35,000 Decisions: The Great Choices of Strategic Leaders." https://go.roberts.edu/leadingedge/the-great-choices-of-strategic-leaders.
[181] Phil 4:13

Ann Lofton, just celebrated that her first born grandson just gave her a first great grandson. We are speaking and believing that this precious little one will be a mighty man of God, that the choices he makes will influence the multitudes for the Kingdom.

I love the beautiful passage in Job that says, "Acquaint now thyself with him, and be at peace: thereby good shall come unto thee. Receive, I pray thee, the law from his mouth and lay up his words in thine heart."[182] Later in that same chapter we are told, "Thou shalt make thy prayer unto him, and he shall hear thee, and thou shalt pay thy vows. Thou shalt also decree a thing, and it shall be established unto thee: and the light shall shine upon thy ways."[183] I have quoted this hundreds and hundreds of times and received results. I love God's Word, because it is who our Heavenly Father is. He *is* His Word.

Jesus said that He only does what the Father does, what the Father tells Him to say and do.[184] The purpose of the Holy Spirit in us is that we would listen to the still, small voice that has promised to lead us. Speak with me Psalm 23 1-3:

---

[182] Job 22:21-22 (KJV)
[183] Job 22:27-28 (KJV)
[184] Jn 5:19

The Lord is my Shepherd and I shall not want.

He maketh me to lie down in green pastures: he leadeth me beside the still waters.

He restoreth my soul: He leadeth me in the paths of righteousness for His name's sake.[185]

Our Father receives pleasure in us speaking and believing His Word, choosing to give voice to His promises, because they are great. Amen!

---

[185] KJV

CHAPTER 17

Women in the Bible

The Bible gives us many stories and teachings about women favored by God. The Lord values women and His Word is full of promises kept and ways He used them powerfully for His Kingdom.

The main purpose of a woman's life during biblical times was to marry and bear children. Barren women sought God's grace, believing that only the Lord had the power to open or close a woman's womb. Psalm 127 speaks of the importance of children as an inheritance of the Lord, noting that the fruit of the womb is his reward.[186] God made many barren women fertile and gave special children to others. Children were the hope of the future, and especially in the Old Testament they were the promise of a strong Hebrew nation that could fight off its enemies.

---

[186] Psalm 127:3

Sarah, as I mentioned in a previous chapter, is one example of our Heavenly Father's faithfulness in this way. She and Abraham waited so long for a child, and the Lord kept His promise to them. Even though Sarah was childless until she was 90 years old, she became the first matriarch of the Hebrew people.

I also told some of Esther's story in a previous chapter, but I must mention her again because she is one of the most recognized Jewish heroines of the Old Testament and she is one of only two women to have a book bearing her name (the other is Ruth). Esther was an orphan girl. The Bible doesn't tell us anything about her parents. Her birth name, Hadassah, means "myrtle", but Esther comes from the Persian word *satarah* which means "star." Esther was a smart and courageous young woman of the tribe of Benjamin. Following the death of Esther's father, her cousin, Mordecai, raised her as his own daughter.

Just like there is prejudice in today's society, there were those in the kingdom who hated Jews. But Mordecai told her that she should not stay quiet about being Jewish. None of us choose our gender, and neither do we choose whether we are black, white, brown, Indian, Italian, Spanish, etc. Some of the folks that hated the Jews included advisors to the king. Esther had stunning beauty, and she was taken into the harem of King Ahasuerus. The king was very attracted to Esther, and did not know that she was Jewish. After he banished his first wife, Queen Vashti, he chose Esther to be his next wife.

As I wrote about earlier, Haman, the king's prime minister, planned to exterminate the Jews. But God used Esther to speak for and rescue her people, and it was Haman and his sons that were hung on the gallows that were built for Mordecai.

The Bible also tells us about women who prophesied. In the book of Judges we are told about Deborah, whose name means "bee", and who was the wife of Lappidoth. Deborah was one of seven Hebrew women in ancient times known as a prophetess. The others were Sarah, Hannah, Abigail, Miriam, Esther, and Huldah. In Old Testament times, women had very little power in society, but God called Deborah to be a judge, prophetess, and warrior.

The Hebrews had been controlled for a long time by a Canaanite group ruled by King Jabon. His general, Sisera, was in charge of a powerful army and underestimated the Hebrews. Deborah told her general, Barak, to gather 10,000 soldiers and take them to Mount Tabor to meet Sisera's army in battle, because God had promised them victory.[187] Deborah was full of empowerment

---

[187] Jgs 4:7

from the Great I Am. When she, full of the faith and power bestowed upon her from her Heavenly Father, began to give orders to General Barak, he said to her, "I will go, but only if you go with me."[188] Deborah said she would, but prophesied that "the journey that thou takest shall not be for thine honor; for the Lord shall sell Sisera into the hand of a woman."[189]

Deborah's prophecy came true, and Deborah and Barak wrote and sang a song about the victory that God had given them. You can read this in Judges 5. Deborah called herself a mother of Israel, and she is an example of strong faith, vision and resolve. When she was called by God to serve her people, she stepped out in courage.

I could write much more about women in the Bible. From Eve, the first woman, to Mary, the mother of our Savior. I also think of the two women who ran and told the disciples with great excitement that Jesus was risen, and that His tomb is empty. The disciples did not believe these women, and thought they were speaking old wives' tales. But God had used them to bring the glorious news of the resurrection!

_____

[188] Jgs 4:8 (NLT)
[189] Jgs 4:9 (NLT)

Don't you just love how our Father loves to show Himself through the lowly of mind and stature, His humble-hearted servants. We speak together Psalm 68:1:

Let God arise, let his enemies be scattered.[190]

He has proved Himself over and over, and against all odds He shows Himself as the Great I Am. He is not in any way bound by any circumstance and wants us, men and women, to know that as well.

---

[190] KJV

CHAPTER 18

Use Your Authority

I love the Fall when we celebrate all those beautiful Jewish holidays and our eyes behold the reds of colorful trees, especially in some of the southern states of our blessed U.S.A. At our fitness club here in Cypress, Texas there are several beautiful, bright, eye-catching, yellow trees. And when we travel to Olathe, Kansas to visit our youngest son it is always very colorful. The Lord's creation speaks of His great power.

Many years ago when our sons were still very small children (John Carlos was eighteen months and Thomas Keith was three years older) the Holy Spirit gave me this amazing scripture from Luke 10:19:

> Behold, I give unto you power to tread on serpents and scorpions, and over all the power of

the enemy: and nothing shall by any means hurt you. (KJV)

I have given you authority to trample on snakes and scorpions and to overcome all the power of the enemy; nothing will harm you. (NIV)

Behold! I have given you authority and power to trample upon serpents and scorpions, and [physical and mental strength and ability] over all the power that the enemy [possesses]; and nothing shall in any way harm you. (AMPC)

The purpose of giving three different translations of this verse is to speak an important truth several times. Our Father and the Lord Jesus Christ and our Divine Helper, the Holy Spirit, have planned, purposed, and preordained that we live as more than conquerors, overcomers living by faith and not by sight.

Take the truth of God's Word. It is your weapon against whatever the attack may be. The Apostle Paul taught that "the weapons of our warfare are not carnal, but mighty through God to the pulling down of strongholds."[191] The above verses remind us that

---

[191] 2 Cor 10:4 (KJV)

"though we walk after the flesh, we do not war after the flesh."[192] We have the power and authority inside of us. We, as confessing believers, are called by the Lord Himself to take the authority He has given us. When we choose to use our authority, we witness our Lord doing amazing things.

Faith is an action word. So if we have faith, we can and should use that faith in who our Lord is inside our hearts to exercise the power of the authority He has freely given us. We should say, *Thank you, my Lord, for this authority that You have given me to take dominion and use the weapons of warfare You have provided all believers.* I John 4:4 tells us the greater one lives in us. You have been given power and authority. Make the wise choice to use what came with the gift of salvation to you.

Once again, I want to be your reminder you are more than a conqueror; you are a child of the Most High God. You are an overcomer. You are called, chosen, one of God's elect. Open up your heart to your Lord and Savior and speak it out loud to yourself. *Thank you, my Lord, that you have told me I am going to have what I say. So I'm saying that I am more than a conqueror. I am an overcomer. My family is very blessed. You do*

---

[192] 2 Cor 10:3 (KJV)

supply our every need. I agree with your Word that you have given me power and authority to love the unlovable, to do good to those who would despitefully use me.

Come with me on this journey of operating in the power and authority that our Father has placed in us. He spoke that out of your belly would flow rivers of Living Water.[193] Not just a river but several rivers. Not just water but Living Water. Pray this simple prayer with me: *Father, I give you thanks for saving me; that Your Holy Spirit arrested me and gave me the knowledge that I was a sinner and that Your blood spilled on the cross is all I need.*

King David spoke truth out loud, in faith, very often. In Psalm 56:3 he said, "What time I am afraid, I will trust in thee."[194] Let us ask ourselves this question: Are we freely trusting in our all-faithful, trustworthy Father? Are we believing in our hearts that He knows our thoughts before we have them? Do we believe that the price for our sins was paid in full at Calvary?

David prayed this simple prayer in Psalm 19:14:"Let the words of my mouth, and the meditation of my heart, be acceptable in Thy sight, O Lord, my strength and my redeemer."[195] What really got my attention with this prayer is that King David spoke to His Father, our

---

[193] John 7:38
[194] KJV
[195] KJV

Father, and mentioned first the words of his mouth. Then he spoke of the meditation of his *heart*. I don't know about you, but I would picture my mind and thoughts when I hear the word "meditation." But David is speaking about his heart meditating on the Lord.

The enemy continually speaks lies — that you are a failure, you are not going to get that job, you are not going to make the grade that will get you into college or trade school etc. Remember what Jesus told us about Satan: he is the father of all lies. We must, as James taught us, continually submit to our Lord, because when we resist the devil he has to flee.[196] What great news!

> Ye are of God, little children and have overcome them: because greater is he that is in you, than he that is in the world.[197]

> Hereby know we that we dwell in him, and he in us, because he hath given us of His Spirit.[198]

We can be confident in the authority our Heavenly Father gives us through the Holy Spirit. His Word is our weapon and we can boldly speak it over our lives as we resist the enemy and claim our Lord's promises.

---

[196] Jas 4:7
[197] 1 Jn 4:4 (KJV)
[198] 1 Jn 4:13 (KJV)

CHAPTER 19

More Than a Conqueror

One night a few years ago, Tom and I turned in quite early, about 9 p.m. I was awakened about 2 a.m. and then again at 2:30. I prayed for a short time, then fell back to sleep, rolling out of bed around 4:30 a.m. because the Holy Spirit was speaking to my heart. "You are going to write a book," He said. The title was to be *You Are More Than a Conqueror*, from Romans 8:37.

My prayer is that you would claim this truth and speak it over your life, trusting in your Heavenly Father to help you live your life according to His will and promises. In this last chapter, I want to leave you with a few reminders about who God is, and who you are in Him.

Our Lord is for us. You can know and believe that our Heavenly Father is ready to give us a greater understanding of His great love, mercy, and grace. I pray that you, dear reader, will receive a revelation that your

Heavenly Father, Creator of the heavens and the earth, is for you. Before the foundations of the earth, He had a book in Heaven all about you. You have never been insignificant to your Heavenly Father. He cherishes and treasures you and yours. Our Lord is determined to get us to where He predestined us to be. He is oh, so faithful to keep us on the potter's wheel, continuing that work of getting rid of spirits that we are not even aware of. Needless to say, He knows us far better than we know ourselves, and is determined to mold and make us into His image and likeness. We have to learn to act out and live out of the image of the new nature that He, our Lord and Savior, Jesus Christ put inside of us at the time of our new birth.

Our Lord wants to give us peace and rest. When we keep our thoughts on who our Lord is, the prophet Isaiah promises, "Thou wilt keep him in perfect peace, whose mind is stayed on thee: because he trusteth in thee."[199] Our Lord Jesus tells us in Matthew 6:25, "Therefore I say unto you, take no thought for your life, what ye shall eat, or what ye shall drink; nor yet for your body, what ye shall put on. Is not the life more than meat, and the body than raiment?"[200] In other words, the author

---

[199] Is 26:3 (KJV)
[200] KJV

and finisher of our faith is telling us not to worry about anything. One of the first Scriptures that was impressed on my heart after receiving the glorious gift of the Holy Spirit was I Peter 5:7: "Casting all your care upon him; for he careth for you."[201]

Our Heavenly Father also wants you to have adequate rest for your body and a supernatural rest for your soul. Hebrews 4 teaches us there is a rest for us believers, having a confidence that all is well because we have positioned ourselves in Christ Jesus. He is our rest. In Him there is a supernatural rest that only His Holy Spirit can and will provide.

Our Lord asks us to love others. We are to love people as the hands and feet of Jesus, His salt and light in the world. I remember many years ago, while growing up in that little Baptist church in Kentucky, we would sing a song called "You Never Mentioned Him to Me." One of the verses went like this:

> You met me day by day and knew I was astray,
>
> Yet never mentioned Him to me.[202]

---

[201] KJV

[202] "You Never Mentioned Him to Me." 2019. Liberty Church of Christ. June 22, 2019. https://libertycofc.org/you-never-mentioned-him-to-me/.

We must live lives that reflect our Lord to others and point them to Him. Romans 5:19 says, "Because one person disobeyed God, many became sinners. But because one other person obeyed God, many will be made righteous."[203] While we were still living in Louisville, Kentucky one of our neighbors, Pat Mears, would sometimes be out in her yard when I would be taking a walk. One day she said to me, "Carlene, how do we practice loving our enemies?" I have thought about that question quite a bit. We are to be in this world, but not of it. We can have a supernatural love for others, even our enemies, if we ask the Holy Spirit to work in us.

Our Lord's Word is our daily bread and a lamp unto our feet. Daily bread means that we need it not just on Sundays or Wednesday nights. His Word is our strength. We do not live by bread alone, "but by every word that proceedeth out of the mouth of God."[204] And Psalm 119:105 tells us, "Thy word is a lamp unto my feet, and a light unto my path."[205]

You are the righteousness of God. The Bible tells us this in 2 Corinthians 5:21. We have this promise through the shed blood of His Son, the Lord Jesus Christ. Precious one, we don't ask our Father for what

---

[203] NLT
[204] Mt 4:4 (KJV)
[205] KJV

He has already given us. You can be very confident that this good work that the Holy Spirit in you has begun, He will perform it until the Day of Jesus Christ.[206] We need to tackle the root of what we believe about ourselves. Do not be captive to a religious system. Enjoy your salvation and the glorious infilling of the Holy Spirit. We should be joyous so other folks will want what we possess.

You were made to shine your light for Him in the world. While at a Barn meeting one Friday, we were praying for all of the many missionaries who have laid their lives down to be obedient to the call of God on their lives. So many different ages, cultures, and colors, yet all laboring in the Kingdom of God where the Lord Himself has planted them. The Holy Spirit in me continues to speak this one word – *light*. He, Christ Jesus, has made us His lights in this dark world.

You were made to be in fellowship with other Believers. I have had many divine appointments on beautiful spring or early summer days, strolling in a park or enjoying the neighborhood pool. I met Jackie Devine for the first time out walking. I also met Charolet, a local swimming instructor. She is a minister of the Gospel alongside her husband, and their son and his wife

---

[206] Phil 1:6

were missionaries in Fairbanks, Alaska for a season. I have connected with many other beautiful, God-honoring, God-fearing people as I am out enjoying the days He has given me. We can be such an encouragement to one another.

Your story and your testimony will make a difference in the Kingdom. I have shared parts of my story in this book, because I want to tell of God's faithfulness and goodness in my life and the life of my family. Oh, how blessed I have been! I pray that the Heavenly Father's work in my life will be a blessing to the next generation, just as I was blessed by the generation before me.

My beautiful, blue-eyed, white-haired, saintly mother is enjoying Heaven now. When she was only a mere twelve-year-old daughter, she came in from school and received the news that her mother had died. This was a traumatic event that was life-altering for my precious mother. I recall one day in my childhood being in the front lawn of the farm house where I grew up. My mother was talking to the three of us girls: me; my sister Peggy, the red head; and Temple, with mother's height and beautiful blue eyes. She said to her three daughters, "Now girls, I married your daddy at sixteen. I didn't have a mom to tell me that I was too young to marry, but you girls do." Her life story was making a difference in our lives.

Temple married at eighteen years to Carl Ruth, a very handsome, brown-eyed, muscular man, and they had two daughters. Their first born was Shirla, a beautiful brown-eyed gal who had two children of her own, Kirstie and Brody. She and her husband, Larry Daniels, are turned-on believers. Larry blows the Shofar every Sunday morning at his church, and also at their home on the hillside in Grayson County, Kentucky. Shirla does a beautiful flag dance. Their two children love and honor the Lord, and so do their beautiful grandchildren. Janall, Temple and Carl's youngest daughter, was married to Bill Baskins. They had no children, and Bill died about six years ago. At our mother's going to heaven ceremony, Temple sat holding her tiny, beautiful great-granddaughter.

Your story, both good times and difficult times, can impact your family and friends for generations. Ask the Lord to use your life to be a blessing and have an impact for His Kingdom.

You are more than a conqueror. This is my heart cry for you for the entire message of this book. This is what the Holy Spirit impressed on my heart when He asked me to write about my life and the things He has taught me about our Heavenly Father.

The longing of my heart for you, whether you be male or female, single, divorced, married, or widowed, young or old, and wherever you are from, is that God, the Father of Abraham, Isaac, and Jacob, would help this truth come alive in you. And that he would reveal Himself to you in multiple ways, for He is the Father of signs and wonders.

You are more than a conqueror. You are an over-comer. You can choose joy. You can choose peace. You can choose Faith. It makes God happy to give us the Kingdom. It is His great pleasure.[207]

My prayer to our Father, in the powerful name of King Jesus, is that in this precious next generation hearts will be turned to the Lord Jesus Christ. That they will have a hunger and a thirst inside of their bellies from the Holy Spirit in spite of peer pressure or mockery. That they will stand firm in their faith in their Savior and be convinced that their Lord is faithful to strengthen them in their walk with Him.

If you are thinking about how you have been rejected many times over, or if you struggle with believing who you are in the Lord Jesus, I want to walk you through a prayer that will bring you peace and freedom. Please pray it with me:

Thank you, Lord Jesus, for loving me and dying on the cross for me. I make this choice

---

[207] Luke 12:32

not just with my mind, will, and emotions but from the heart. I repent for allowing this spirit of rejection to have a hold on me, and I choose now to renounce it. It can no longer be a part of me. I believe You are who You say You are. Help me to know more each day who You have called me to be and what Your plan is for my life. Thank you, Lord Jesus, for setting me free. I love you, Father God, for setting me free and I will share with others how they can be free and walk in a much greater peace with the joy of the Lord. Thank you that in you, I am more than a conqueror. Amen.

About the Author

C arlene is a passionate minister, intercessor, and prophetic evangelist who has dedicated her life to spreading the love and power of God through a variety of impactful ministries. Raised in rural Litchfield, Kentucky, Carlene's journey of faith began at a young age, with a calling to serve God that became evident when she was just four years old. Her zeal for ministry led her to teach Sunday school and work with Christian youth during her teenage years. Longing to expand her horizons, she moved to Louisville at 18, started a career in cosmetology, and devoted herself to God's work before eventually stepping into full-time ministry.

Throughout her journey, Carlene served as National Advisor for AFIRE Ministries USA and contributed to the growth of ministries like AGLOW and FLAME, in addition to leading her own ministry, Jesus is Truth Ministry. She has been an unwavering advocate for sound doctrine, faith-based teaching, and God's love, demonstrating her steadfast commitment to the Great Commission. Carlene's passion for empowering others through faith took her across Kentucky and beyond, speaking at churches, revivals, and seminars, and sharing God's message of hope and transformation.

In 1979, Pastor W.L. Rodgers invited Carlene to host a radio program, where she delivered God's word through a weekly broadcast on WJCR 90.1 FM in Louisville. This opportunity enabled her to connect with a larger audience, and her ministry flourished with engagements both domestically and internationally. She traveled to places like Israel, South Korea, Ukraine, and Mexico, bringing the message of God's love, salvation, and healing to countless individuals.

Carlene's deep faith and dedication to spreading God's word has touched the lives of many. Her unwavering belief in God's call led her to embrace every opportunity presented, trusting fully in the Lord's plan for her life. Today, she continues her mission as a minister, speaker, and leader of Jesus is Truth Ministry, sharing her message through *You Are More Than a Conqueror*.

www.ingramcontent.com/pod-product-compliance
Lightning Source LLC
Chambersburg PA
CBHW072010040426
42447CB00009B/1570